Angels

ARE EVERY WHERE

Angels

ARE EVERY WHERE

WHO'S YOUR ANGEL?

GEORGE FULLER

To order additional copies of this book, contact:
Xlibris
1-888-795-4274
www.Xlibris.com
Orders@Xlibris.com
762455

CONTENTS

INTRODUCTION

M OST OF US have religious views and beliefs. Some believe that their religion is by far the perfect one. Most people are not inclined to others' religious concepts or beliefs. Therefore, they somehow downplay others. Baptists think Methodists are not as good, and Muslims and Jewish descendants have been at odds for centuries, so have Jehovah's Witnesses and Mormons. One can get into a very heated debate on the topic. So what does one do to support such a claim? They turn to other resources such as their ministers, preachers, and rabbis. This somehow adds value to their belief system and gives their claim more credibility. This gives the opposition more fuel to aid in the discussion of what religion is superior. I'm not knocking anyone's religious beliefs. I try to understand each to help broaden my knowledge on the subject. I personally regard mine as mine and subsequently go with that.

Some of the dialogues that come from such discussion are the following: Is God real, or is there a place called heaven? If God created heaven and earth, who created God? Does He look like us? What race is He? Does He have human flesh? There are many that don't believe (atheists), and historically, they were some of the most brilliant minds to walk the earth.

Everything in this book is based on my personal journey in developing my faith. There will be no scriptures to support anything written. This is a common-man belief system and the situations and circumstances that have occurred throughout my lifetime to support my belief system. These events have had a dramatic influence on me. One thing is for sure: I'm not trying to convert you to change anything you believe in. It is my hope that after reading this book, you'll be able to identify the angels in your life and give them the recognition they deserve. Sometimes your angel may not know they were your angel. If you are lucky, maybe they are still alive. If not, give God the recognition for supplying them in the first place. Angels in this book have passed on.

It is written that God created heaven and hell and everything within. It is said that there are angels both in heaven and hell. Those angels that were disobedient to God were cast into hell as punishment. There is not a lot of discussion about angels. They do exist. I believe that there are three tiers of angels:

1. *Heavenly angels.* Heavenly angels are, of course, in heaven. They carry out the task that God wants them to perform. I believe that when one is about to succumb to death, these angels come to take your soul to heaven.

2. *Guardian angels.* Guardian angels are with you on a daily basis. They protect you. Sometimes they whisper words of wisdom or words of warning—warning that something is about to happen so that you will be prepared to deal with the event or situation, clearly giving out advice if you are listening. Are you listening? If you fail to heed their instructions or advice, they simply designate an earthly angel to intervene.

3. *Earthly angels.* Earthly angels are here on earth. They are of flesh. They could be a loved one or, maybe, a total stranger. Sometimes you may be in disarray or confused as to what avenue to take. They give you clarity, directions, or instructions on how to deal with whatever the issue may be. They are there to aid you in your spiritual development or fulfillment. For some of us, that may take a lifetime. But they are there to keep the progression moving forward until you reach a certain understanding and maturity that allow the next level to begin.

Holy Spirit—it is as it's named, a spirit. It's not of flesh. It's not human. It is a spirit. Mystical. Powerful. Graceful. Personally speaking, when the Holy Spirit comes into my presence, there is peacefulness, a calmness, and a deep relaxing feeling that you can't resist but, on the other hand, just embrace and hope will last forever. This feeling penetrates deep within your soul, and you don't want it to end. Sometimes I'm not aware that the Holy Spirit is in me. This feeling is so incredible that you won't resist. You don't want it to end. Everything around you is secondary. You have just received the Holy Spirit and all of its blessings. The Holy Spirit will guide you to what it wants you to do or say. I'm not aware of the words that flow out of my mouth, but I know that my lips are moving. The Holy Spirit is in control, and I'm just the messenger who will deliver the message it wants. My behavior and body movement will be dictated by the Holy Spirit. I believe and have experienced the Holy Spirit present itself and prepare me to be introduced to God. I believe that when God wants to talk to me, He sends the Holy Spirit ahead to prepare me for His presence so I won't be overwhelmed by His presence but instead be grateful and conscious that He loves me and I'm special to Him.

I have had many encounters with the Holy Spirit, and it wasn't until after my spiritual development that I knew what was going on. Beforehand, I was spiritually dead. In other words, when I grew spiritually, God allowed me to see and understand what I had experienced even though I was not aware of what was happening during that time. To be in the presence of the Holy Spirit is a powerful moment in itself, and I appreciate God for allowing me the opportunity and the patience to understand His many blessings.

All the angels I mention in this book could very well be the same. That being said, my purpose is to divide them into groups so that the reader can easily identify which was present in my life. Make no mistake about the Holy Spirit. The Holy Spirit is *the* Holy Spirit. I believe the Holy Spirit approaches us in many different ways. Maybe our personality has something to do with it. I'm just saying.

The next time you are in a crowd, see if you can pick out your earthly angels. Could you identify them even though you know they are right in front of you? Would it make sense to treat your fellow man with kindness and respect? Understand that one can discover who your angels are or have been. You will come to the realization that those angels were put here by God for you. I looked to the past to discover who my angels were. My goal is to seek them out and let them know who they were and give them the recognition and appreciation they deserve. I want to do this to give God the praise for being there for a sinner like me. No one would do that for me, and after all these years, He stuck it out with me even though I was spiritually dead for a long time. Thank You, Father, for letting me see the goodness and grace You've given me.

SUGAR HILL

T O BEGIN THIS journey, we must establish a time frame. The year was 1956. There were numerous events occurring globally. Dwight D. Eisenhower was president. There was a young man from Tennessee that would become a rock-and-roll legend for generations to come. His name, by the way, is Elvis Presley. This was a time when the civil rights movement was on the upswing to generate awareness to the inequalities of people of color and specifically African Americans, known at that time as Negroes. These injustices were happening not only in America but also several continents away in South Africa. It was a time for public demonstrations, freedom marches, and a rebellion against Jim Crow laws, which affected minorities. Both blacks and whites united to bring these much-needed changes to the forefront. These laws were designed to degrade, humiliate, and depress the economic climate of those whom the laws were clearly intended for. These laws were created by our Congress and Senate. State and federal laws were enforced by all levels of government. A lot of these laws encouraged segregation. Imagine not being able to sit where you wanted on a public bus but in an area designated Coloreds Only. Maybe you were hungry, and instead of entering the restaurant from the front, you had to place your order at the back or side because of the color of your skin. This is how it was even though you paid the same dollar value as whites.

The school systems in many states supported segregation especially in the southern states where black people were denied access. Most of the books were used. The part that really had a dramatic effect on me was to see the young white kids from the north come south to help in voter registration. They believed in America and believed in democracy and tried to make things better from a civil rights point of view. What a lot of people don't know or are not aware of is a lot of people lost their lives behind these injustices and were brutally beaten, just like the ones they were trying to help. Those injustices really needed to be changed, and a lot of innocent people lost their lives behind the struggle. It didn't matter if you were from mainstream America or a small town. You were affected deeply. It mentally had a direct impact on how you thought and how you lived under these circumstances. It seemed as if the laws and conditional mind-set of that genre were still applicable today. It was based on the premise that as a black individual, you were and still inferior to whites. If you were fortunate to be alive or be a part of our American history then and didn't sustain any physical/bodily damage, count your blessings. Many of us were not that fortunate.

Sugar Hill is a small segregated community located 2.5 miles northeast of Roxboro township. What I remember about the place is there were twenty-three houses on about fifteen acres of land. This property was owned by my grandfather William Whitfield, better known as Badge Whitfield. I affectionately called him Papa Badge. Papa Badge was a rugged man of six feet tall, and at the time of my introduction to the world, he weighed around 260 pounds. He was extremely dark-skinned and had only one good eye. I never asked him what the history behind the lost eye was. I never asked him what happened out of fear. And it didn't matter since I would always be there to see for him. The lost eye was gray in color. His voice was very distinguished in that it was raspy and coarse. Papa Badge was around sixty-five years old. Papa Badge had a charismatic personality and was wise beyond his years. He had a fifth-year education and, like a lot of men during that generation, had to quit school early to help support their families. They didn't complain because it was expected of them for survival.

Papa Badge was a carpenter by trade. He possessed leadership qualities that made people want to follow him. People would seek him out when they needed advice or consultation on different subjects. He would always give them the time and energy to help resolve the problems. Papa Badge built these low-income houses with the help of his son William Whitfield Jr., who was called Pap. Pap was also very dark-skinned and was at least six feet four inches tall. He was athletically

GEORGE FULLER

built but wasn't the sharpest knife in the drawer. He was, however, a lot of fun to be around. Sometimes some of Papa Badge's church friends, who were also carpenters, would come by to help and to just hang out with him. They all had a common history and enjoyed being around one another.

Papa Badge's house was in the middle of the acreage and was on a hill that allowed him the view of the area. I lived with Papa Badge until I was ten years old. My mom, Peggy Fuller, bought one of Papa Badge's houses even though she was his daughter. Talk about being independent. These houses had no indoor plumbing or air-conditioning as we have today. These houses were constructed over a half century ago. Even then, he had a waiting list. In our little community, we had our own store, a church, a baseball field, and numerous basketball goals. We also had a well that served the entire community with fresh water. We were poor, but most African Americans were around that time.

The most important part of the community was the church, which is currently in service today but at a new location. During that era, it was common to have services twice a month because most preachers had two churches. Our church schedule were on the second and fourth Sundays. Papa Badge was not a member of the neighborhood church. He was a member of a local church. Papa Badge would go to church every Sunday. He rotated to churches depending on what Sunday it was. Guess who was with him? That's right—me. It didn't take long for me to realize that Papa Badge was very popular at all these churches. Sitting there watching and listening, I had questions begin to enter my mind. *Who is this man everybody in church keeps talking about? Why are they talking about Him? Why do they keep chanting "I love the Lord"? Who is He? Why are they standing up and telling others about what God and the Lord has done for them?* They are saying that God was there when they needed Him most. As a very young lad, I begin to look around the church to see when these two fellows were going to show up. I learned later on that they were testifying.

That following Monday morning, Papa Badge and I had been working for a long time. He decided to take a break and walked over to a stack of two by fours and sat down. Like most kids that idealize someone, I sat as close to him as I could. Without thinking about it, I would mimic his body language, wanting to be just like him. As we sat there, and without looking directly at him, I asked him, "Where is God's home?" Staring straight ahead, I could see him out of my right eye. Papa Badge turned toward me with a wide smile on his face—a proud look. Suddenly, I felt his huge hand on my shoulder, pulling me closer to him—a hug for sure.

He said, "God lives in heaven. Heaven is a special place. God created heaven, a place not of this world. A place where we can live with Him after we die. If you live your life the right way, God will reward you, and that reward is to live with Him forever in heaven." He continued to say that as I got older, I would understand more about God and His goodness and His love for me. "Don't worry yourself about things you don't quite understand now. In time you will."

I said to myself that Papa Badge loves God and thinks the world of Him. I guess I will too. I can remember back as far as age four prior to starting school, I would follow Papa Badge around when he was working. Papa Badge was the father I never had. I would get him the tools, supplies, food, and water when he got thirsty. Papa Badge would construct these low-income houses starting in March through November. He could build two or during the time. Occasionally he would work over the winter depending on how much it took to complete the task. It was exciting to see new families move in—more friends to make. The families on Sugar Hill got along pretty good. There was not a lot of drama. We looked out for one another. We helped one another, and those stay-at-home mothers always watched out for the working mothers' children. They had no problem disciplining you when you got out of line. Back then, we called a spanking a whooping. *Time-out* is a phrase that the current generation came up with. When you got a whooping, you remembered clearly because you just didn't get one, say, from the stay-at-home mother but also when the real mother got home and got the news that you needed to be disciplined.

It was twice as bad as the first one. The reason was that mothers felt that you and your bad behavior embarrassed her, and you would pay the price. We did have some cracker-barrel types, and we knew who they were. Even though they lived in the fast lanes, they looked after their homes first.

BRIAN MAYO

I T WAS EARLY June of 1955 when I first met Brian Mayo. Papa Badge and I had finished working on one of his houses. We were on our way back home when I noticed this young lad running in his front yard. What really got my attention were the sounds he was making. They didn't make any sense to me. He seemed to be enjoying himself, however. I didn't understand those strange noises that came from him. I looked at Papa Badge, and he looked at me and replied, "The boy is retarded."

I said, "What is retarded, Papa Badge?" We were not politically correct during that time. It was what it was. However, he didn't learn as quickly as other people. He did things to get attention. I continued to look back at him as we continued to walk home.

Papa Badge said, "Maybe you should play with him sometimes. None of the other kids will."

I said, "Maybe tomorrow."

The next day, I noticed the young boy again outside playing in the yard, playing by himself. He was at least a foot taller and outweighed me by fifty pounds. I was maybe four feet tall and not an ounce over sixty pounds. He was a couple of years older with a medium-brown complexion. His hair was cut very short and seemed to roll tight to his scalp—in other words, *nappy.* That afternoon, I walked over to his front yard where he was playing. I walked up to him and said, "I'm George. Can I play with you?"

He replied, "Yeah." For some strange reason, as he was saying his last name, he prolonged the last part and began to bobble his head as he was doing so. He said, "My name is Brian Mayo-yo-yo-yo-yo Mayo." He said it again, "I'm Brian Mayo-yoo-yoo-yoo-yoo Mayo," as if I didn't hear him the first time. I thought, *What is wrong with this guy?* Then it dawned on me what Papa Badge said. He was slow. So we started playing. I did whatever Brian wanted to do, and he was enjoying all of it.

Later on that afternoon, I overheard one of Papa Badge's friend make the comment, "The boy is retarded." When I heard the comment, I didn't like the sound of it, and I got mad. He was making fun of my new friend. Every day after that, I would go over to Brian's house, and we would play until dark. We did all kinds of stuff, like seeing who could run to a particular designation the fastest. Sometimes we would find some tobacco sticks, and we would tie a piece of rope at one of the ends and pretend it was a horse. We would put the sticks between our legs. We would ride the sticks like a horse as fast as we could, turn, and stop suddenly, forcing the tail end to slide along the ground. This action created a tailspin, which would create a lot of dust. That was fun to see how much dust we could make. We had connected and liked playing together.

One day, while we were playing, I saw the Anderson boys coming toward us. They had a bad reputation in the neighborhood as troublemakers. They had to pass by us to get to their house. As they got closer, I could hear them chanting, "George is playing with the retard." They kept repeating it, laughing all the time as they were saying it. Terry was the little fat one. Jamie was skinny. They fed off each other's behavior as brothers do. When they got within a couple feet and stopped, I knew they were going to rub it in. In the corner of my eye, I saw a stick on the ground that was a couple feet long. I dared Terry to say it again. He did. As soon as the word parted his lips, I quickly reached down and picked the stick up and started hitting Terry across the head as fast and hard as I could. When Jerry saw what was going on, he took off. I kept hitting Terry as many times as I could with no mercy in sight. He started running to avoid me hitting him. I ran with him while continuing to pound the stick to his head and body. I simply lost it. I had never been this mad before.

All of a sudden, I heard this voice calling my name, "Jim, stop." It was Papa Badge's voice. I stopped hitting Terry. I knew the voice and stopped immediately. That was when I noticed Terry was bleeding from the head area. He was bleeding from the barrage of blows I hit him with.

Papa Badge said, "Jim, come here!" Jim was the nickname Papa Badge gave me. Why, I don't know. I just assumed it and let it go at that. If that was what he wanted to call me, it was OK.

Papa Badge and some of his friends were sitting on the front porch and had witnessed everything. Our house was directly across from Brian's. As I passed by Brian, I saw that he was crying. It hurt to see him crying. He didn't deserve to be made fun of. For me, I knew what was going to happen. I was going to get a whooping. For some strange reason, I didn't care. I protected my friend and wasn't going to let people make fun of him because he was slow. I knew that I was going to get a whooping in front of all of Papa Badge's friends. They were going to laugh at me.

As I got closer to the front porch, I stopped. Looking at Papa Badge, I asked, "Do you want me to go in the woods and get some switches, Papa Badge?" Switches are long branches from a fully grown tree that are tied together. When struck with these switches, not only is it painful, but it also leaves marks on the area as well. He didn't answer my question.

He said, "Come here." When I reached the bottom step, I realized that I had done something that Papa Badge didn't approve of. I had embarrassed him in front of his friends. I began to cry. I didn't mean to embarrass him. I could not look at him. I lowered my head in shame. As I got within his reach, I felt his hand lift my chin up to where I could see him. He said, "You can't beat up everybody that says something bad to or about your friends. Let your friends fight for themselves. What you did was honorable. I'm proud of you for sticking up for Brian, but let Brian stick up for himself from now on. Now, what I want you to do is go down to the Andersons' house and tell them that you are sorry and that you won't do this again."

As I turned to do what Papa Badge had said, one of his friends whispered to Papa Badge, "That boy knows what to do with a stick! That was some pretty work," laughing as he was commenting. On the way to the Andersons' house, I noticed that some of the neighbors had seen what had happened and were interested in what was going to happen next. They had this wry look about them.

As I approached the Andersons' yard, I could see Mrs. Anderson was holding Terry on her lap while nursing his wounded head. When she saw me, she hollered out, "What the hell do you want? You did a terrible thing to my son! You are a mean boy. Why on earth would you do such a thing?"

I said, "Mrs. Anderson, they were making fun of Brian. They were calling him a retard. Papa Badge told me to come down here and for me to say that I was sorry. It won't happen again."

She replied, "You are Badge Whitfield's grandson?

I said, "Yes, ma'am." Mrs. Anderson and the neighborhood knew the history with Brian. She didn't like the idea of her sons saying such things.

She said, "My boys told me something different, and they lied." She said, "Boys, come on in the house. You are going to get it now." That meant they were going to get a whooping. Getting two in one day was bad but better them than me!

The next day, when I saw Brian, he said something that surprised me. It was as clear as a bell. He said, "George, you are my friend." There was no bobbling of the head or the prolonged ending that usually comes with the last word of his sentences. Our friendship blossomed after that day, and I really enjoyed being around him. Looking back, I realized a couple of things. One is that you can create a reputation without looking for one. If you were my friend, I wouldn't let people do something mean to you. People like it when someone stands up for the underdog per se. The neighbors and Papa Badge saw this, and me being small in size said more than words could describe. After that incident, the other kids in the neighborhood started to come out and play with us. That was what I always wanted but didn't know how to make happen. It happened on its own.

It was the third week of August. Brian and I were playing on the woodpile Papa Badge and Uncle Pap had made. We were jumping off it, just having fun. What was about to happen next, I didn't see coming. When I jumped off the pile of wood, I landed on a two by four that had a five penny nail sticking straight up. I didn't see it coming. When I landed on it, it went through my foot about an inch behind my big toe and the second toe. The pain was unbearable. To see the blood squirting from my foot was so painful. All I could do was scream as loud and as uncontrollable as I could. As I fell to the ground, Brian noticed what had happened and began to scream louder than I did. We were both screaming hysterically! The pain was unbearable. I screamed at Brian to go get Papa Badge as I cupped my foot in my hands. I passed out!

When I regained consciousness, Papa Badged was holding me on his lap on the front porch. He had placed an old sock around the injury to help keep blood from dripping all over the place. He called out to May. That was what he called my grandmother, Mary Whitfield. "Go down to the seller and get a slab of fatback." A seller is a storage area for meat such as hams, which are to be eaten at a later date. Other meats such as sausages and tenderloins can also be stored there. Fatback is the part of the hog's backside that doesn't have a lot of lean meat to it. Back in the day, fatback was used as a cooking additive, especially in vegetables.

When Grandma May returned with the fatback, Papa Badge wrapped it around my foot where the nail had left a hole. The fatback was used to shrink the hole and help fight off infection. It did a good job. It didn't help with the pain and soreness that followed. I was off my feet for two weeks.

The first day of school arrived, and it was a painful day at best. The last thing I needed was to wear a pair of brand-new shoes, as I was still recovering from a severe foot injury. On top of that, we had to walk three miles to get there and three miles back. The only good thing was that it was warm. The state was paving the highway in the neighborhood, so the bus wouldn't be available until construction was over. That morning, over twenty students converged at the bus stop to begin our journey to school, me included. As we walked, I began to lag behind. These new shoes and the tenderness from my injury was making it hard to keep up. I was still in a lot of pain. But I had to try. You only go to first grade once, and you definitely don't want to miss the first day of school. As I drifted backward from the group, Brian never left my side. Brian could see the pain I was in, so he suggested something. He said, "George, I'll be your horse. You can ride me to school." He bent over, and I didn't hesitate to jump on his back. When the other kids saw what was happening, they joined in.

When we reached Main Street, this car driven by an elderly black man slowed down and came to a stop. You didn't see a lot of black people with a car during that time, so he got a lot of looks, to say the least. This black man said to us, "Why are carrying the little boy on your back? Is this some kind of game?" By then all the kids had gathered around the car, and they began to tell him what happened to me. He said that he couldn't take all of us but would take the little one and a couple more. I quickly asked if Brian could be one of them, and he said yes. A black man with a car—he must be doing all right for himself. As we were riding, this man started asking questions like where we lived. Everybody in the car said Sugar Hill at the same time. He then asked if we knew Badge Whitfield.

Brian answered immediately, "Yes, that's his grandpa," pointing at me.

The man looked at me and then said, "Yeah, I saw you with Badge at church last Sunday. Everywhere Badge went, you never let him out of your sight. You were closer to him than a necktie is to a white shirt. I looked up, and you were sitting in the deacons' section with Badge. Kids are not allowed to be up there. But if that's where Badge wants his grandson to be, so be it."

It took the state two weeks to finish paving the road. During that time, the kids in the neighborhood took turns giving me a ride to and from school. They made a contest of it. They would see who could carry me the farthest. Sometimes they would fall to the ground from exhaustion, trying to outdo each other. It was fun for them, and I loved the fact that they really cared about me. How am I going to repay them for the kindness they had shown and given me?

FIRST GRADE

F IRST GRADE WAS not what I expected it to be, nor did I have any idea what to expect. Up until now, all I wanted to do was have fun with my friends. Learning to read and write as well as arithmetic was a lot to incorporate in my young mind. This was about as boring as learning to tie my shoes. It took a month to figure it out, and afterward, it was OK. For me, the best part about school was that I knew the weekend was coming, and Papa Badge and I would go to church on Sunday. That was what I really missed. It was exciting for me to be in service and hear Papa Badge urge with enthusiasm the preacher to, in his word, preach. He also said the phrase, "God is good." Sometimes he would belt out, "I love the Lord." Other members would also participate. At the end of the sermon, the preacher would ask Papa Badge to render a song for the congregation. As if it were on cue, he would stand up and start. "Give Me That Old-Time Religion" was his song of choice. Papa Badge would start out with "Give me that old-time religion, / Give me that old-time religion, / It's good enough for me." Each verse was slightly higher than the first one. The verses overlapped until it got to *me*, which was substituted for *mother*, then *brother*, then *father*, and then *sister*. Every church we went to, Papa Badge was asked to sing this song. The congregation knew what to expect and would sing along with Papa Badge even though they had heard it forever. That was amazing to me.

This rotation of churches happened with the help of Uncle Roosevelt, who carried us to and from church. He was one of a few black people who had transportation. We were blessed. Sometimes when Papa Badge would sing his favorite song, Uncle Roosevelt would join in. Now Uncle Roosevelt had a deep bass voice and stood six feet six inches tall. There was no mistaking who he was. They knew how to work a congregation, and they loved every minute of it together. There were tricks they knew that would get the audience engaged or get them to participate. These tricks were passed down by other singers or by just observing others perform. You want the audience to be engaged because that means you and the audience have connected. Uncle Roosevelt had a gospel quartet called the Silver Moon Quartet. When we would go to the local church, the quartet would meet us there, and when asked to sing a song, they would back up Papa Badge and it was on. They could really sing. They knew when to come in and out of verses and let Papa Badge take charge, and he (Papa Badge) knew how to push the right buttons to make them perform to perfection. They could turn an audience upside down with their harmonies and melodies. I loved to hear them sing.

Back then, we didn't say *sing*. We said *sang* if you were really good. They were awesome! Apparently Papa Badge had taught them the tools of the trade. You could see the respect that each member showed Papa Badge as they were singing. They looked to him for approval, and he would always give them the nod. That means you are on point, and they would sing their hearts out. Sometimes on a Sunday evening, we would go to a local church that had a gospel program. Church committees would invite local groups to come and participate on these programs. This was one way of raising funds for the church and enjoying an evening of music. There could be as many as fifteen or more groups, and each one had a theme song plus three other songs during the set. Back then, most quartets sing a cappella—without instruments. If a group had a guitar, that was fine, and the church piano was available to all. There were four voice ranges that made up the Silver Moon Quartet: bass, baritone, tenor, and lead. Each member could sing in each of the voices, and that made a strong group. They had versatility and harmony that most groups didn't have. They were the group to compete against, and you better bring your A game. On these programs, the group really showed why they were the best around. On Wednesday nights, they would practice at Uncle Roosevelt's house. They would rehearse the songs they were going to sing the following Sunday. My cousin Marvin Nelson and I would sit and watch as the group would arrange songs. They would then practice each song until it was perfect and each member was satisfied with the results. They would collaborate on the voice that would lead and who would sing the other voices needed to make the song complete. Afterward they coordinated on what apparel was to be worn and what song they would sing if an encore was needed. After practice, they would sit around and laugh and talk about past events or experiences they shared. That was great. I miss that even today.

DECEMBER 10, 1956

THIS WAS THE most crucial day of my existence. This day, an innocent young boy had to face the realities of the world. This was a day of learning, but most of all, the months that followed were of suffering. This day was in the forefront of my faith—the beginning of my personal connection to God. This day is why I'm writing this book. It is my sole purpose of sharing my testimony to my God for allowing me to live this long to share with you my experiences.

This experience didn't start on the tenth of December but the night before after supper. My mom went into our room, and I went in to plead my case. She looked at me and said, "I know that look. What do you want?"

I said that tomorrow Papa Badge was going to kill hogs. I was wondering if I could skip school so I could be here to see Papa Badge's sisters and brothers. They always came to help out, and it would be nice to see them, kind of like a family reunion. She said OK but warned me that this was the last time. I said thanks and went into the living room to watch TV with Papa Badge. Of course, I had to tell him the good news. He smiled. I was so excited. After a couple of *Bonanza* episodes, I was off to bed. Lying there, I knew that they always killed hogs in the winter months because the weather acted as a refrigerator for some of the meats. Men would do the killing, and women would clean, cook, and prep the meats for storage. The food was what I liked. Oh, it was going to be a great day. I could feel the excitement in the air. What I didn't tell my mom was that I really wanted to be around Papa Badge. School had interrupted our time together.

The next morning, when I woke up, I noticed how cold the room was. We had one potbellied stove in the middle room, and the other rooms like the kitchen and Papa Badge's room had stoves. Our room didn't. I always laid out what I was going to wear next to the bed.

Quickly I redressed and headed straight to the middle room, where there would be heat! When I entered the room, the potbellied stove was blazing, and the room was completely warm. This room was large enough to hold a full sofa, a TV stand, and a TV, plus six to eight chairs. East of the middle room was the kitchen. West of the middle room was Papa Badge and Grandma Ma's room. West of their room was the front porch. Now north of Papa Badge's room was the fancy room. This room was reserved for special guests like the preacher and his wife and deacons and their wives that visited. The furniture was top-notch—two sofa chairs, four end tables with lamps, and a center table with a Bible on it. A special cloth covered the center table. I was not allowed to play in this room. Underneath the kitchen was the seller that I mentioned earlier. Outside and south of the house fifty yards away was the hogpen. At that time, we had four hogs.

When I entered the room, Papa Badge was all smiles. I greeted all the relatives with a good morning, calling out each one in succession. First was Papa Badge, Uncle Pap, Uncle Roosevelt, and Uncle Charlie. Then I greeted Papa Badge's two sisters, Aunt Mary and Aunt Sara. All of them said together, "Good morning, George," poking fun at me. I laughed too. I got me a spot around the stove, and like most kids, I did what I saw the grown-ups do—each one of the uncles would reach out toward the stove as if they were warming their hands, which should have been warm already. It was a gesture that made no sense to me, but I did it anyway. I guess it may have been a way of collecting their thoughts as they talked, or it may have something that relatives did and, like me, copied or passed on to the next generation. About the time we all got really comfortable, Grandma Ma yelled out, "Breakfast is ready." We all got up and headed to the kitchen. Papa Badge sat at the head of the table. I sat next to him on his right. Across from me was Uncle Charlie, and beside him was Uncle Roosevelt. Beside him was Aunt Mary. Beside me was Grandma Ma, followed by Aunt Sara. Uncle Pap sat at the other end of the table, facing Papa Badge. Papa Badge led the grace, and when he finished, he leaned over to me and said that someday I would have to say grace before every meal. He chuckled.

As we were eating, Papa Badge told everybody that I was going to meet Louisiana. I said, "Who's Louisiana?" All the relatives started laughing. He poured a tablespoon of coffee from his cup and placed it in my mouth for me to swallow. I was thinking that this was all right. I always wanted to drink some coffee, and now Papa Badge was thinking like me. When the coffee hit my tongue, it was so strong that I felt like my brain exploded in my head. Tears were running down my cheeks without me doing anything. Boy, this coffee was strong. I tried to swallow some of it, and what got down my throat began to come back up. I started coughing it back up, which didn't help, but it was more of a natural reaction on my part. When I got my breath, everybody at the table fell out laughing at me. Papa Badge leaned over and said, "You just met Louisiana." Papa Badge had played a joke on me. Once I caught my breath, I started laughing too, even more than them. I must have looked really stupid, but in the back of my mind, I knew that all of them probably had the same joke played on them.

As soon as the sun came up, we all headed to the hogpen. We were prepping the area for what was about to come—the actual killing of our quest, the hogs. First on the agenda was the scalding trough. The scalding trough was a big oval pot long enough to hold the hog after it was shot. This trough had a fire burning underneath it to heat the water it contained. This boiling water would soften the hog's hair so that removal would be easier. They would roll or turn the hog so all the boiling water had touched the entire hog, and they let it lay there for a while to soften the hair. Removal of the hog's hair was done by using knives, and the most effective way was with a jar top. They simply scraped it off. Secondly, wooden planks were placed side by side to accommodate the width and length of the hog, and hair removal happened here. After all the hair was removed, the hog was then hung up on the tripod, where the hog was sliced from head to toe. The inner parts of the hog were removed and placed into buckets or some cooking utensils for cleaning and then storage. Depending on the parts, some were used for cooking. My role was to carry what I could inside the house to the women, and they knew what to do. After the tripod, the hog was then placed back on the slabs to be cut by sections, such as shoulders, rump, and midsection. Each section produced certain foods that we eat today without giving it much thought. The outer skin makes, say, fatback or my favorite crackling, which also could be turned into lard. Intestines could be turned into chitterlings. Ground-up shoulders could be turned into BBQ, sausage, or tenderloin. This list could go on, but I think I will stop now. When the grinding and cutting was completed, the sections were placed into the seller. Most meats were salted down for preservation and prepared for consumption at a later date.

After all the preliminaries were done, it was time. Uncle Roosevelt was in charge of the weapons. He handed Papa Badge the rifle, and he took dead aim at one of the hogs and fired, hitting the hog in the head. The hog fell immediately to the ground, and the uncles jumped into the pen. One held the prize by head while the other slit the hog's throat. Then they let the hog bleed out, and while that was occurring, they congratulated Papa Badge on what a great shot he made. Of course, the testosterone was running high, and bragging rights were up for grabs. This was a contest on who could kill the hogs on the first try. Macho men. As the hog lay bleeding out, my mind reflected back on the days when Papa Badge and I would go around to some of the neighbors, gathering up slop. Slop is the remains of the meals that no one eat or sometimes the peeling of vegetables or meats that humans found distasteful but hogs really like. A lot of times, when we were carrying slop from the house, the buckets had water in them, and it would spill on my pants. The smell was a fragrance that wasn't pleasing to one's sense of smell. It was awful to say the least. Plus the nasty liquids or solids would get on your clothing, and you looked terrible. I quickly learned to carry those buckets without wasting a drop. This day was what all the carrying and feeding was all about.

As the day continued, I ran errands from the hogpen to the house. Later on in the afternoon, I went into the middle room, where Aunt Mary and Sara were sitting next to the big potbellied stove. The fire had died out, and the room was cold. My two aunts were pretty old, in the upper eighties, and for that reason or some other, they decided not to remake a fire. I would guess that they were waiting for the men to return. That was OK. I would make one but decided to go into

Papa Badge's room instead. I didn't want them to see me, so I closed the door. It was going to be a surprise after I got it going. When I entered the room, I began looking for the items I would need such as kindling, small pieces of wood, kerosene, and of course, matches. I found everything I needed and started to place the wood in the stove. In my clumsiness, I wasted a large amount of kerosene on the cotton flannel shirt that I was wearing. Holding the matchstick box close to my side in my left hand, I pulled the match toward me with the right hand. It ignited. I was on fire! Within a second, I went up in flames. I knew I was in trouble because I became paralyzed and I couldn't move. I could see myself running and rolling on the ground. I could not move. Everything began to slow down. I tried to scream, but no sound came out. I tried to move but couldn't. The flames were up to my head by now, and in that moment, I knew I was going to die! In my mind, I said these words: *God, I'm only five years old. Please don't let me die.* I passed out.

When I regained consciousness, I was in the hospital some five or six miles from home. Papa Badge had put a sheet around my wounded side and was holding me in his arms like a baby. That was when it dawned on me that the pain I was feeling came from the accident. It was unbearable, to put it mildly. It seemed that the worse the pain got, my mind would click in and out, and I would pass out. I was in and out of consciousness a lot. When I was conscious, I noticed everything going on around me. This was the first time I had been in a hospital. My two uncles sat close to Papa Badge with the look of worry of losing me on their faces. It was like all of them could feel the pain I was dealing with, and they kept talking to me even though I couldn't remember a thing they said. I passed out. I could smell my burned skin. I had never smelled anything like it before. The closest I could compare it would be like the smell of a piece of burned meat. I had smelled burned meat a lot while I was learning to cook, and it was far worse than that. Human flesh was different. As Papa Badge was holding me, I could feel the blisters forming on my side. They would balloon out and burst when filled with pus. They kept moving the sheet around me to find a dry spot to absorb the pus I was discharging. The pain was unbearable, and again, I passed out. This time, when I returned, I noticed that the people who came out of this room were not dealing with the pain I was going through. Some of them were smiling. One other thing I noticed was that they were white. Papa Badge kept asking the nurse, "When are you going to see my boy?" She kind of played him off and went about what she was doing. I was saying to myself, *Yeah, what about me?* I knew that this place was supposed to do something for me. I just didn't understand when and what. Papa Badge kept on carrying me around and would ask several nurses about when I would see a doctor. Finally this one nurse looked Papa Badge in the eye and said, "You know, niggas always see the doctors after white people." The look on Papa Badge's face said a lot. It was a look that I had never seen before. He was humiliated by the remark—saddened, mad, frustrated. After this day, I would see this look a lot in my friends. That one word changed the expression on Papa Badge's face dramatically. He looked devastated and without any way to help me when I needed it the most. It made me feel even worse because of it and how it impacted Papa Badge's demeanor. I was curious as to how this one word changed his demeanor.

We returned to the waiting area, and Papa Badge began rocking me back and forth. I could sense from him that if something wasn't done soon, he might lose me. I looked up at him and said I was going to be all right, even though the pain had increased and I could barely get it out. I had to tell him. He just looked at me in disbelief. Finally we got to go in the other room where the doctor was waiting. He began to ask questions about what happened as he removed the sheet from around me. When he saw the damage of my burn, he walked away momentarily. He then told Papa Badge that there was not much he could do because technology was not advanced enough in this area of medicine at this time. However, in a couple of years, I could get a skin draft if it was healed by then, and that would be costly. As he wrapped adhesive tape around me, he continued to tell us that the burn was the worst he had ever seen in his forty years of practicing medicine. He said that the heat burns ranging from my stomach to within one inch of my spine was devastating. He continued to say that the amount of heat and its intensity would have a dramatic effect on the inner organs like my

GEORGE FULLER

intestines, underarm, heart, and lungs. They would shrink based on the amount of heat that had penetrated throughout my body. He said that I might not develop into the man size I might have been destined to be. More bad news followed. He also stressed the fact that because of the burn under my right armpit, I wouldn't have full range of motion in that arm. When he finished wrapping me with the tape, he began to apologize for the lack of things he could do.

Papa Badge said to him, "Doc, you did what you could, and we thank you for that."

Then the doctor said something that has always been in my mind. He said, "Mr. Whitfield, if you are in the area, please give me a call to let me know how he's doing." He then gave Papa Badge a card. When Papa Badge picked me up and turned around to leave the room, I noticed the doctor had sat down on the bed, and he was about to cry.

On the way home, I regained consciousness again, and I just had to ask Papa Badge what a *nigga* was. The moment the question was asked, both uncles and Papa Badge fell out laughing. It didn't seem funny back at the hospital. I was confused. They laughed all the way home. When we arrived and got out of the car, I could hear some singing from inside the house. The song they were singing was one that I heard at one of Papa Badge's friend's funeral. I realized that they didn't believe I was going to live through this. My two uncles rushed to open the door as Papa Badge carried me inside. He laid me down on the large sofa and quickly had Grandma Ma get a sheet to cover me. The house was full of people from the neighborhood, and they were singing some song that I had heard at one of the funerals Papa Badge had attended. I guess they were putting the dirt on me. My mom was going out of her mind with guilt, saying things like her only son was going to die and she should have made me go to school that day and it was her fault. I was still in an incredible amount of pain and continued to go in and out. It seemed that when I returned, the singing got more intense. It made me feel even worse. Papa Badge came over to the sofa and whispered to me that he was going to get me some help. "When I return, I'll tell you what a nigga is," he said. I nodded and passed out. When I returned to consciousness, the room of people were still singing, and some of the elders were crying along with my mom. For some reason, I knew that I wasn't going to die.

After a while, the outside door opened, and Papa Badge came into the room with this man, a strange man in strange clothes. He was carrying what I learned later were herbs. Papa Badge called Grandma Ma to come. He said, "Ma, come here," and she was there in a flash.

She said, "What are we going to do, Bro. Badge?"

He said, "We are going to do whatever it takes to get Jim back on his feet."

He told her to boil the herbs, and he and this strange man would be in the kitchen in a few minutes to help her. Then Papa Badge told the people in the room to leave and come back tomorrow. He and this strange man had some work to do. The people left, and I was happy for once on this terrible day. I really wanted to tell them that I knew I was going to be all right. When I asked God for His help, He came and rescued me. That was the last thing I remembered while I was burning. Now, I kind of understood why Papa Badge went to church every Sunday. There was something special about the one called God or Jesus. Everybody left the room. This strange man walked over to where I was lying and looked directly at me. It was a look that said, *There is nothing to be afraid of. I'm here to help.* He then smiled and began to pour this grasslike substance, which I learned later was sage and pine shavings made into an ornament he had brought with him. He then lit the substances so it would catch fire. He began to fan the smoke, filling the room with this fragrance. This substance gave off a strange scent that I had never smelled before. As the smoke began to fill the room, he began to chant words of another language. This chant was powerful in that the minute he started, I didn't feel the unbearable pain that had been inside of me over the last four hours. As he continued to chant these phrases, I slowly drifted into sleep.

When I returned from sleep, the strange man was gone. Papa Badge had pulled up a chair next to the sofa. When I looked up at him, he began to smile. That worried look was gone, and he had returned to himself. He told Grandma Ma that he and I were going to talk about what the word *nigga* meant and how we were going to deal with the wounds. He said to me, "Now, white folks came up with that word to describe black people. It is not said to elevate you but to demoralize your spirits, your self-esteem, and how you see yourself. They want you to think that they are better than you simply because of the color of your skin. Most of the white people around here are prejudiced and resent or hate the sight of you. I don't want you to grow up hating people because of the color of their skin. Nothing comes from hate but hate. As you grow up and begin to be around people of different races or colors, religions, countries, and backgrounds, find out what you have in common. If a person is of another race, don't reject him/her because of it. Reject them because of their behavior or attitude toward you. Then move on. If someone calls you a nigga, you may want to fight them for the intent they are pointing at you. Sometimes that may be necessary, but choose your battles. Do not let the battle choose you. If you treat people the way you want to be treated, with respect, then you must give them that, and if they don't return it, walk away. If you can't walk away, demand it through knowledge/wisdom, not your fist. You can't beat the world up. You may not understand all of what I'm saying, but in time, it will come back to you, and in the meantime, just think of how you want to carry yourself in the future. It will all work out. Trust me. Now rise up so I can remove the bandages the doctor put on you."

As he cut them off, he had another clean sheet to wrap around me. He wanted me to turn the sheet around once the pus had accumulated and move it to a dry spot. He said, "Do this as long as you are up." In the morning, he would see how it looks, and if the blistering had stopped, we would start using the medicine he and the strange man made. He said that the next day, he and Uncle Roosevelt would go uptown and get some things I would need for my burn. My mom and Grandma Ma came into the room to check on me and tried to lift my spirits up, and soon, I was in the room alone. I tried to find a comfortable position to sleep on but was aware that my right arm could not come into contact with the burned area. When my arm would touch the burned area, it would stick, causing more pain and damage to the area. It was going to take some getting used to. As I lay there, the pain returned, and like most of the day, I was in and out all night.

The next day, when Papa Badge and Uncle Roosevelt returned from town, Papa Badge removed the sheets to see how I was recovering. He said the blistering had stopped. He asked, "How do you feel, son?" I told him my insides were still burning. Now that I had time to reflect on the condition my body was in, I can acknowledge the fact that because of the intensity of the heat, it had to find a way to exit my body. The left side seemed to be the path. When I touched the left side, it was almost as hot as the original side. It was so hot that once I touched it, I had to remove my hand quickly. He told Uncle Roosevelt that the sheet was almost dry and that was a good sign. He said that he would give it a few more hours, and after supper, he would start the treatment. Then Grandma Ma brought me some food, and for the last twenty-four hours, I finally ate. I was so weak from the pain and exhaustion I really needed a good meal, and Grandma Ma could lay it down in the kitchen.

After supper, Papa Badge started his treatment. He said, "Jim, you are probably going to have to retake the first grade because this is going to take some time. I don't know how long. We'll just have to see." He removed the sheet and placed a fresh towel on the wound. With hands as big and rugged as his, I could barely feel his touch. But he was touching me because I could see him. He was gentle as he removed the excess burned skin away. He took an enormous amount of time in tending to the area. After the skin was removed, he used a light paintbrush to spread the sass on the wound until it was completely covered. Sass was a combination of herbs and spices he and the strange man made. Then he addressed the upper right arm and armpit. No matter how gentle he touched it, it hurt. I tried not to show him, but he could see the tears as they fell below my cheeks. I never said a word or cried out when he was doing all he could do to help me. I had to bear it. I did it to myself. I was suffering, and there was no end in sight. When he finished, he said that he would have to remove the sass every few hours during the night and day. He wanted the wound to be dressed often to keep fresh sass on it.

After a week, the pain had begun to subside some. I began to ask questions that had been on my mind about the accident. The first was, What happened? Papa Badge said, "Brian came running to me and said that you were on fire. So we all ran into the house, and you were laying on the floor. Your shirt was still smoking when we got there. You had passed out. We then rushed you to the hospital."

My next question was, Who was the strange man that came with him on the day we got back from the hospital? He said his name, but it was a Native American name, and I couldn't remember what it was. He said that he was a medicine man. He was a Native American from the northeast side of the county. He said that his father was a slave who ran away the plantation and this tribe gave him refuge. I could understand that because we shared the same common hatred for whites. So when you see a black person that may have white traits, that doesn't mean that the white settlers impregnated their women. It could be that Native Americans were more likely to integrate with blacks than whites. That was the history during that time. The white settlers were fighting the Natives or indigenous people because they wanted control and ownership of the land. He said, "Now your grandmother is part Native or indigenous people. She was born and raised up in the Mebane area." Mebane is a small town located about an hour's drive from Roxboro.

My last question was, If Brian came to my rescue, why hasn't he come by to see me? All the other kids have. Papa Badge said that Brian was traumatized by what he saw. He said, "He was shaking like a leaf on a tree when he got us. He was screaming so loud that his best friend is dead. Most of the neighborhood heard him. He just kept hollering, 'George is dead! George is dead!' I told Charlie to get him while Pap and Roosevelt and I got you."

Brian never came to see me after that. They moved a little after my accident. It would be years before we would meet again.

After lying on that sofa for five months, my side had finally healed. I suffered daily, and now I could resume living again. On the first day of school, I entered the classroom to an applause. All the students knew of my injuries and rewarded me for such. In small towns, everybody knew everybody's business. It was nice of them. Little did I know during this time of suffering that my teacher and Papa Badge knew each other through church, and she had heard about my accident and extended her hand to help. She kept him up on my studies. It was fun to go to school with Papa Badge.

Weekends came around, and the weather allowed Papa Badge to go uptown as part of his routine. First stop was at Wilson's Market. Mr. Wilson was an elderly white man about the same age as Papa Badge. He was the owner of the store. On this particular Saturday, one of Papa Badge's friends, Mr. Cousins, was there. Mr. Cousins often came by the house and helped with building some of the houses we were working on. Mr. Cousins was a big dark-skinned man like Papa Badge. The three of them would always congregate at the back end of the store and shuck and jive with one another. They liked joking around at one another. As we were all standing there, Papa Badge gave Mr. Cousins the eye. That meant something was about to happen, and it did. Papa Badge looked at Mr. Wilson with as serious a look as he could and asked him, "Mr. Wilson, which one of us is blacker?" Mr. Wilson looked at Papa Badge and then looked at Mr. Cousins then back and forth again to make sure he got this right. Before he could give them his answer, they both started laughing at him, and then he realized that it was a joke. He started laughing too after he saw what was going on.

He said, "Badge, you really got me." Then they started mocking how he was looking at the two of them, and all of them continued to laugh.

The next stop was Tom's Auto Supply Store to see Mr. Taylor. I think Papa Badge loved talking to Mr. Taylor. The first time I saw Mr. Taylor, I thought he was white. You just don't see that many of us with really light skin complexion. Plus, this man had the largest hands I'd ever seen. They also went a long way back. Whenever Mr. Taylor came over to Sugar Hill to visit relatives, he would stop by to see Papa Badge. I liked being around the two of them. Whenever they talked in what I called Hebrew, they say one thing, but it carried another meaning, and it was as if they competed to see how many phrases they could come up with. They always laughed at the meaning of each phrase even though I didn't have a clue as to what they were saying. They just enjoyed each other's company.

GEORGE FULLER

BULLIES

BULLIES ARE PEOPLE who go out of their way to intimidate others physical, verbally, psychologically, or emotionally. These tactics are applied when the bully thinks they have more advantage to be successful.

It was the third week of the new school year. I was playing on the playground that morning, and I had noticed this boy named Reggie Brown bullying one of the guys. He always wanted to show off, and one of the things he liked doing was beating guys up, taking their lunch money, and laughing at them. I knew that one day he was going to try me because, let's face it, I was not a big guy. I tried to avoid him. That morning, that didn't happen. He walked toward me. The playground was full of students, and I just knew what was going to happen by the look in his eyes. When he got within arm's reach, I started hitting him with all I had in the stomach. I threw a barrage of licks on him until he fell to his knees. I continued to hit him in the face or wherever I could hit him. One of the students had ran to the principal's office and got the principal, Mr. Talley. Mr. Talley was at least seven feet tall. When he got to us, I was still hitting Reggie. I was scared that if he got up, things might not be so good for me. When Mr. Talley snatched me off him, I felt relieved. I knew that it was over. He reached down and grabbed Reggie and stood him up. He said, "Come with me."

We followed him to the principal's office, where he sat us down. The first question was, Who started it? I pointed to Reggie, and he didn't say a word. He looked at Reggie and said, "This is the last time you will come in here."

I said to myself, *What does that mean?*

He told Reggie, "Instead of fighting him, you should be protecting him from bigger guys trying to start a fight with him. You see that he is a lot smaller than you, and you two should be looking after each other instead of fighting each other. Do you two understand?"

We both said yes at the same time.

He added, "George, you know Reggie is always getting into trouble. When you see him about to do something stupid, you should tell him to stop. Think about it. You should tell him, 'We don't want to go to the principal's office again.' If one of you come in here for any reason, I'm going to bring the other one in, and both of you will get a whooping. What that means is you two better look out for each other. Reggie, go in the next room and drop your pants."

He followed him in, and the sound of licks he was putting on his backside was loud. It was hurting me to hear them. Reggie was screaming out with each blow. It must have been at least ten. When he finished, Reggie came out in tears. He wouldn't look at me. Then Mr. Talley said, "George, come in here and drop your pants."

When I entered the room, I noticed the paddle (Ping-Pong) he was using, and I had heard about the holes in it. Why were there holes? Each time a blow was administered, the holes would suck the meat into hole, causing more pain. He hit me like three times on each cheek and told me to return to class. I didn't cry, but I knew that sitting down was not going to happen that day. My buttocks were throbbing and burning like crazy. The next time I saw Reggie, he gave a wry smile, but we both knew that we had to do what Mr. Talley said. If someone looked at me funny and Reggie was around, he didn't hesitate to challenge them. I, on the other hand, kept a close eye on him too. If I saw or thought he was going to do something to get him in trouble, I would remind him of our pact, and he would always calm down. We remained that way throughout grade school. We got to be each other's guardian angels, and along the way, I met another friend. Years later, after we had grown up, we would see each other from time to time. We always had a respect for each other, and it showed years later. We just enjoyed each other's company. We continued to look after each other when possible. It lasted until his passing a few years later.

GEORGE FULLER

RECOVERY

I T WAS LATE afternoon in July when I saw one of my childhood friends, Daniel Jones, throw a rubber ball against the house. Papa Badge and my two uncles were sitting on the front porch. I was sitting on the steps close by. When Daniel spotted me, he walked over and asked if I wanted to play catch. Of course, I said yes, so I got up, and we were throwing the ball back and forth to each other. After about four throws, I heard that familiar voice call my name. I said to myself, *What have I done now?* "Jim, come here!" called Papa Badge. The sound of his voice had a sense of urgency about it, and I reacted that way. I almost ran into him as I approached him. He asked, "Does your arm or shoulder hurt when you are throwing?" Confused as to why he was asking me that question, I simply shook my head from side to side. "Do you hurt at all?" he asked. I continued to shake my head. Then he said, "Raise your shirt up." When I got the shirt about shoulder-high, he quickly finished taking it off for me. He then began to examine the burned area, which I had forgotten about. He began to rub it gently and asked if it hurt.

"No, Papa Badge," I replied.

"Are you sure?" he asked.

Then he put a little bit more pressure on the area between the armpit and the part of the triceps muscle that was attached to it. This area was severely damaged during the fire, and if not healed properly, I would not be able to lift my arms straight up. Apparently it was OK. Papa Badge looked at Uncle Roosevelt and said, "We need to take Jim back to see the doctor tomorrow. Can you call him and let me know what time?"

The next day, we went to the doctor's office. The doctor was glad to see us. The expression on his face was in no way like the last time I saw him.

"Well, young man, sit up on this table, and let's see what we got." Papa Badge and Uncle Roosevelt stepped back so the doctor could do what needed to be done. Like Papa Badge, he started rubbing the burned area, pinching it and asking questions. "Does it hurt?" he would ask. Then he would rub it in a rough manner and again asked if it hurt. I said no to all the questions. Finally he said, "Raise your arms up." He wanted me to rotate my arms and shoulder in a circle. Then he drilled me with all kinds of movements so many times I couldn't remember. When he finally finished, he looked over at Papa Badge and said, "What did you do?"

Papa Badge told him about the strange man and the sass they made. Then he told him that he would clean the area anywhere at least six to eight times a day for the last four and a half months. The doctor just looked at Papa Badge with amazement. He said, "I had heard of these homemade remedies, but I never thought I would witness one. If someone comes to me with a burn, I'll be looking for you." They all laughed, and we left.

Papa Badge was strutting like a peacock. He was so proud of what he had done and rightfully so. I was proud too, and Uncle Roosevelt was proud. When we got into the car, Papa Badge told Uncle Roosevelt that he wanted to go to Sam's house. He said, "Jim, we are going to see Sam."

I said, "OK. I've been there before."

Papa Badge turned around quickly in the seat and looked at me with this surprised look on his face. He didn't say anything but just looked.

When we arrived, Papa Badge told Uncle Roosevelt to stop the car. Papa Badge began to tell me that a long time ago, the white settlers were afraid of the Natives and fought them over land. To make the long story short, after the white settlers got control of the situation, they isolated these people to reservations so the government could manage how they lived. Those that didn't meet the government demands were killed or incarcerated. When we walked up to the strange man's house, there was a little girl about my age sitting on the steps. She was very pretty. Her long hair hung well below her shoulders and was as black as coal. What made me not forget her were those big brown, hazel eyes. As we were standing there, she gave a little wave as if to say hello. So I waved back.

Of course, I smiled. At that moment, the door opened, and this strange man came out smiling. When he got to us, Papa Badge began to explain what the doctor said, and they both shook hands. He asked Papa Badge if he could see the area that sustained the damage. Papa Badge didn't hesitate to tell me to lift up my shirt in front of a large group of people that had gathered. I wasn't surprised that people gathered around us. Strange people in the neighborhood often attract a crowd. That's what we do when someone new comes in the neighborhood—we check them out to see why they are there. Before I could finish taking my shirt off, this strange man finished for me. Like all of them, he began to touch and feel the burned area. When he had done his examination, he looked at me and said that I was a lucky young man. I nodded and put my shirt back on, because when some of the people saw my burn, they began to say awful things. Papa Badge and the strange man had walked off to themselves. They were talking and laughing, but I couldn't make out what they were saying. I did hear Papa Badge call the strange man Sam.

As we walked back to the car to leave, I stopped and turned around and said, "Mr. Sam, thank you for helping me." I got in the car, and when I looked at those people, I knew that they knew that Mr. Sam did something extraordinary for me. I will always be appreciative to Mr. Sam for his gift of life and love.

Now that I've had time to reflect on that terrible day, my mind always go directly to the nurse on duty that day. Imagine that your child just received the most devastating burn possible. This child's hot body is so close to you that you can feel the heat trying to escape his fragile little body. All you can do is to try to comfort him in any way you can. You need to comfort him. There are not a lot of options left. This child, your child, is screaming at the top of their lungs for you to help him, twisting and turning, clawing and begging for you to make the pain go away. I remembered the look in his eye just like it was yesterday. When I think about the nurse, maybe she is a mother, maybe not. What I do struggle with is how one can see a child in that condition and not do anything due to the fact that that poor little boy is black.

MARK WILLIAMS

I MET MARK Williams in the year 1963. It was one of the most historical years in United States history. The war in Vietnam was escalating. There were protests against the war and civil rights. Later on that year, Martin Luther King Jr. delivered the "I have a dream" speech in Washington, DC. In November, the United States president John F. Kennedy was assassinated. The country was in transition due to political and civil unrest. However, there was this group from Liverpool that had taken the country by storm called the Beatles. James Brown was at the forefront, and this recording company in Detroit known as Motown was producing one hit after another.

My mom and his worked at a local dry cleaner. They walked to and from work together. They (Williams) lived in a big house on the upper half of Sugar Hill. They had one sister named Carol and three brothers, Fredrick, Kendrick, and Sheldon. Sheldon was the oldest and had moved to New York after graduation. As we began to get to know one another, he said that his father had passed on some years ago. It didn't matter because I didn't have one either. Papa Badge was the only father I knew, and that was good enough for me. He smiled when I told him. What I liked about him was that when he competed against me when we played basketball or football, he was so serious. He was so fiery. His passion for the games we played was sometimes funny to me. It was just a game, for crying out loud. As only fate could conjure up, the more we were around each other, the more we bonded. As the friendship developed, they moved across the field from us, and I didn't have to take the long walk up to his house and he didn't have to take the long walk down to mine. Perfect. We played backyard sports. We never played anything remotely close to organized games. We had our own team and would go up to the upper half of Sugar Hill and play against them in football and basketball. On our team were my two cousins,

Mark, and me. The opposition consisted of four players from the upper half of Sugar Hill. All of them were older and larger. When we played football, we had to gang-tackle them to get them on the ground. We went at it. We won some and lost some. It was very competitive and fun. Mark and I really connected so well that we decided to start wearing the same clothes like twins. We both would scheme on the mothers to buy certain things that we wanted in order to be just alike. It worked out pretty good. In the summer, I started mowing our neighbor's yards just to make money to buy my own clothes. By the end of summer, I had acquired more than fifteen yards that was mowed every two weeks like clockwork. I was doing it. I didn't see Mark except on the weekends. We usually went to a movie or house party. At the parties, he would always do his interpretation of his idol Mr. James Brown. He had all the moves down pat, but the one thing missing was he could not sing even a little, not one note. However, this did make him popular among the opposite sex.

One day, after seeing just how much clothes we had accumulated, I asked him how he was making money. He replied, "Pulling tobacco." I had heard of this but never ventured out to find out what exactly he did. He said that he would show me next year. He also said that he made six dollars a day, and over the week it was about thirty dollars. He was also off on weekends. That was more than what I got for mowing all those yards—a lot more. He said Thomas showed him how to do it. Thomas was a natural-born leader and knew how to hustle. Being one of eight kids, he was about making money and was stubbornly independent, traits that I always liked about him. He was also very talented in a variety of things. He was ahead of his time in some regard. He could make things from nothing.

The best Christmas I had ever experienced was with my homeboys. One night, we had all met at the Joneses' house after school break. That night, Thomas asked, "What are you guys going to get for Christmas?" All of us said nothing. He said he had an idea for us. He asked us to meet him at his house the next day, and he would reveal what he was thinking. The next morning, we met. He said that we were going to make homemade go-carts. We burst out laughing. Really? We continued to giggle and poked a little fun at him. He looked at us with a fierce look in his eyes. He said, "Are you with me or not?" We kind of looked at one another and kind of agreed to hear this joke out. He said, "We are going over to the landfill, and when we get there, we will be looking for plywood boards, tricycle wheels, and rope. Now if we find what we need, George, I need you to ask Papa Badge if we can use some of his tools."

I said, "Yeah, I'll ask him." I was still kind of laughing, and the others were too. I was thinking that I would just go along with the program. We all were thinking the same thing. So off we went. When we got to the landfill, we began to change our minds because we began thinking what it would be like if this worked. So I thought, *Let's give it a shot.*

As we looked through the junk, we found some plywood that may work as a seat. We asked Thomas for his approval. He would reject or accept whatever we showed him, and before long, we found two plywood boards. Then we found some rope. Next were the tricycle wheels. We found eight of them in about an hour of looking, and he said, "I think we got what we need." We returned to his house, and I found Papa Badge and asked if we could use some of his tools.

He said, "For what?" I replied that Thomas had this idea for us to make homemade go-carts. He started laughing too. He finally agreed but said that I was responsible for their return. I agreed as he handed me tools he thought we might need. He continued to laugh and said, "This is going to be something. I'm going to be watching you guys."

Thomas took over, and we did whatever he told us. Around two o'clock, we finished the first one. We were so excited and wanted to test-drive. Thomas said no. We needed to finish the second one before dark, which would be between five and five thirty. Just before dark, the second one was complete. Then he said that we should go home and eat.

"Why?" we asked. We wanted to ride.

"We'll have time for that later, but we have to get our chores done, or you know what that means," Thomas said.

"Yeah, we know."

"Be back around eight o'clock, and tell your parents where you will be," he said.

We said, "OK."

After we did what we needed to, we met again. Even though it was dark, we found light next to the well. It was always lit because Papa Badge had a streetlight placed near the well so people could see how to get water in the dark. Thomas rechecked everything and said that he and Mark, his older brother, would take the first one down the road. This road was on a steep hill, which was perfect for a downhill drive. They took off and, when they got to the bottom, pulled the cart back up the hill for the run. Then he told me and Mark to take the second one down. We jumped on, and down the hill we went. Man, that was so exciting and a thrill to be riding. We returned to the top of the hill, and we all were grinning and overflowing with joy. Thomas made it work! We never laughed at him about his ideas again. He was just beaming with pride, and we were just elated that this idea was on time for Christmas. I got everything this Christmas, and it was still the best ever.

The following year, as promised, Mark got me a job with him and the Jones boys, Thomas and Daniel. He showed how to prime tobacco as he said he would. I made more money at twelve years old and no longer had to ask my mom for anything. I had enough lunch money for the year. Can you say independent contractor? I was more confident or cocky than ever in my life.

The next year, changes were in the horizon. The previous year, one of the farmers we worked for told me we were the fastest tobacco primers he had ever hired to work for him. What he didn't know was that we were racing, and the one that finished first that day would get a dollar from the other three and bragging rights. My strategy was to start on the second row. This position would help increase your time to and from the slide. You didn't want to be on the slide row simply because it would slow you down. The footing was not the best because it usually had clumps of dirt in them in the row. Plus the driver was going to stay back for the slowest primer.

Each time you finished a row, everyone rotated to the next row. We didn't realize at the time that it would all come out equal at the end no matter how fast you were. One morning, we all met at the hill where farmers would come by to hire primers. We liked to work together and would if someone needed four primers. If not, we would go with whomever for the day. Two white farmers pulled up about the same time, and one yelled out the pay for a day's work. The first one hollered out, "I'll pay six dollars a day! I need four primers."

I yelled back, "We got that last year!" The next farmer also needed four primers and jumped on that price by increasing the pay to seven dollars. I yelled back that I was hungry and asked if he served breakfast. Before he could answer, the first farmer said that he would pay eight dollars and serve breakfast and dinner. We all ran and jumped on the back of the truck, leaving the other farmer wondering what just happened. We didn't care what his thoughts were. We knew what we were getting, and we were happy.

As we were riding down the road, Thomas looked at me rather strangely and said, "You know what? You are crazy," with a wry smile on his face.

I said, "Yeah, you are right, but I got us more money plus two meals." Then, out of blue, I said, "Shit, my mom can't cook worth a damn! She don't get much practice working two jobs. The only good meal I get is when I go up to Papa Badge's house." They started laughing like crazy. I must have sounded pretty desperate. I realized that those farmers had a small window to get the crop in before school starts and before fall kicks in with dew. We continued to do this every summer until I was sixteen when I got my driver's license.

Miss Williams passed on the next spring, and Mark and I drifted apart. Shortly after her passing, Mark's older brother Sheldon was killed in a car wreck in New York. I knew the brothers and his sister went to go to New York for the funeral and to say goodbye to their brother. I also knew that it really hurt Mark a lot. He always talked about how he and Sheldon had the same features and looks. After Sheldon's death, Mark quit school, and when I went looking for him, I couldn't find him. I heard that he had got in with the wrong crowd and was drinking a lot. I so desperately wanted to see him and just talk to him, but I knew that there was nothing I could do to bring his mom and his brother back. What would I say? If anything, what could I do for him? I felt so helpless. One night, I was sitting in the living room doing homework when I heard a knock on the door. When I answered it, it was Mark. I was so glad to see him. He was also happy to see me too. We went into the living room, and I was like, "Where on earth have you been? It's been at least three or four months since I've seen you."

Then he said something that I will never forget. With his head lowered as if he were praying, he said, "George, I feel so lost at times that I don't know what to do. I mean, when you lose your mom, it's hard to deal with things." After all, he was the firstborn. He continued, "It almost killed her when Sheldon passed. We couldn't afford to have his body brought back for his funeral here, and we didn't have the money to go to New York for his funeral. Mom just couldn't take losing him, and I think that was why she died suddenly. The whole family is suffering, and we don't know what to do." As he continued to talk, I could see the tears flowing down his face and meeting underneath his chin. His voice was beginning to crack as his words were stumbling out of his mouth. My heart was breaking in half to see my friend in so much pain and agony.

As I looked at him, something began to change. As we sat there, something very strange or odd began to unfold. Suddenly the lights began to dim lower. As Mark continued to speak, this very warm, comforting feeling surrounded me, and even though Mark was speaking, it was like he was at a distance, but I could hear him in the background. This presence made me feel so relaxed—relaxed like I had never felt before—but I was not intimidated or afraid of this moment. I just accepted it as it was. Then this "voice" whispered in my ear, "He won't be around long. There's nothing you can do." This voice was calming, but the tone was firm but gentle. I realized that Mark was going to die. Then as quickly as it came, this powerful, relaxing presence that surrounded me was gone in a blink. I somehow came back to normal and continued to listen to my friend. This was the first time I had experienced being in the presence of the Holy Angel. I also believed that God spoke to me for the first time. I was so spiritually dead that I wasn't even aware that something this special was happening to me, preparing me for that which was about to come. Mark said that if he was living with us, things would be different. He wanted to ask my mom if he could come and stay with us but knew she couldn't take care of the two of us. We were just as poor as they were. It would be a burden on her.

"Don't ask her either. Please keep this between us," he said. Then he said something that really surprised me. He said that he was going to be a father at fifteen years old.

I said, "Who's the mother?"

He said, "Susan." Susan was Thomas's second-oldest sister.

He got up and headed to the door. As he was making his way to the door, he said that he told her that he would come by and that was where he was going. His last words before he went out of the door was "I still don't know what I'm going to do." I didn't say anything because this voice didn't want me to say anything. I knew it and believed that, and I felt it when the feeling came over me. When we got to the door, we hugged each other, and then he was out.

That night, as I lay in bed thinking about what had happened and what was said, I couldn't get this feeling that surrounded me out of my mind. I didn't understand it and what it was or why it happened. A couple of days went by, and I realized that we needed fresh water. So I grabbed the bucket and headed to the well at the Jacksons. As I approached the well, I saw Susan there. I said to myself, *Why would she come this far to get water when Papa Badge's well is about twenty yards from their house?* This was strange. As I got closer, she turned and looked at me. I could see she had been or was still crying. She said, "Mark was killed last night in a car wreck on Highway 49." He and about six others were in the car. Mark was the only one that didn't make it. She said it was true. She asked me if I was going to the funeral because she was. I said no. I wanted to remember him as he was. I put my arms around her, and we began to cry for our friend.

A few days after Mark's funeral, I went up to Papa Badge for supper. As we ate, he started talking about my friendship with Mark. I guess it was showing on my face that I was having a hard time with his death. I began to tell him about the visit from Mark and some of the things he

GEORGE FULLER

spoke of. I didn't tell him about the feeling that was present that night, however. When I finished, he said something that made me think even more about what had happened. He said, "Sometimes God does things that we don't understand, and we have to be patient, and the answer will come sometimes unexpectedly. If he said that he felt lost at times, well, maybe God didn't want him to be that way and decided to bring him home to be with him. Maybe that's how you should look at it." I think that's how I will look at it from now on.

Whenever I'm in the area where they laid him to rest, I always stop by to spend some time with my friend. Rest in peace. You may be gone, but I will never forget you. The way I looked at it was that something special happened to me simply because I knew that after the fire, someone in heaven was looking over me. Now the list just got larger. I don't know why I kept that special time to myself. Now in reflection of it all, that was the first time God had spoken to me. Was God working on me then? Was He preparing me for something?

MR. MOORE AND MS. FORD

I T WAS DURING my senior year of 1969 when decisions had to be made on how I would approach life after graduation. In the later part of 1968, I had passed all requirements for the armed forces. That afternoon, at the end of testing, we were told to go into one of the rooms and wait for instructions. After ten minutes, a staff sergeant came in. He had all the test results and chose one to read from. He said that the list of names were the ones that passed, and they would be notified through the draft board when they would have to report for active duty. He said, "I'm going to cut through the chase and give it to you straight. You are going to be trained for combat in Vietnam. You will report to a location for eight weeks of basic training followed by eight weeks AIT, or advanced infantry training." The names were called, and mine was the second one called. My knees buckled, and I almost lost my breath. Once the list was completed, we were told to report to the bus to be transported back to our original destination—Roxboro.

On the bus ride back, there was absolute silence all the way home. Like most of us on the bus, we knew that life was about to change dramatically. We could lose our lives in a matter of months. I couldn't get my mind around the thought that I could be dead right after my eighteenth birthday. I kept up with the news because it interested me to know what was going on in the world. I had seen the numbers for American fatalities, missing in actions, and those injured. I had never held a gun in my hands before, and now they expected me to kill another human being who had done nothing to me. Questions began to race through my mind. Why were we fighting for the rights of other people half a world away when there was so much work to be resolved here? How many more lives would have to be lost for this war to end? None of this made sense to me. If we were the dominant country in the world, why didn't we practice what we preached? Talk about contradictory. As I lay in bed that night, I tried to come up with the pros and cons about the war. One thing I wanted before I was inducted was a car. How would I obtain such a high goal? It was during my last year in high school that I started driving the school bus for extra income. I did this even though I knew that after graduation I would have no control of the destination I was about to embark on. If I were to go to Vietnam, I wanted to own my own car before I leave.

It was early one January morning when I suddenly heard this soft, gentle voice whisper to me right after I woke up. It said, "Go to the local cotton mill." I got up and followed the voice. The local cotton mill was a couple of miles away. That morning, the weather was briskly cold. I had to walk. I was so cold when I arrived. I had to give it a try. When I arrived, I spotted a young black man outside the facility taking a smoke break.

I approached him and asked, "Where do I put in an application?" He pointed me in the direction of the personnel office. When I entered the room, there was a young white lady sitting behind a desk.

She looked up and said, "May I help you?"

I responded, "I'm here to put in an application." She said that I would have to do that Monday through Friday, eight to four. She was very professional in the way she spoke to me.

As I turned to walk out of the door, I stopped and said, "Ma'am, this is the only chance I'll get. I'm still in school, and when I get out, your office is closed. Besides, I don't know that many people that own a car or would get off work to pick me up from school and bring me down here." She looked at me as if she was trying to figure out what to do. Finally she said that it would be OK, but I would have to hurry. As I was completing the paperwork, this big middle-aged white man with silver-gray hair entered the room. His office was adjacent to hers. The moment he entered the room, I could see the lady become very tense. I knew immediately that she was in trouble. I felt bad for her. He walked over to the window, looked out for a minute, and asked me if I was finished.

"Yes, sir," I said nervously.

He said, "I'm Mr. Baker, the plant manager. Why don't you step inside my office?"

"Mr. Baker, I wasn't trying to get her into trouble," I said, looking directly toward her. He replied that she wasn't in trouble.

When we got inside his office, he began to interview me while looking at the application. He then asked, "Where do you see yourself in five years at this company?" My reply was "Sir, three weeks ago, I passed the armed forces test. They told me that after graduation, I would receive my draft notice where I would have to report and the date that I would have to report. Once I complete basic and advanced training, I would more than likely be sent to Vietnam. I may not make it back, but before I go, I want to have my first car."

I'm thinking that he was in the military by the look on his face. Maybe he knew someone who was—a family member. Maybe the ending wasn't good judging by the sadness that came over his face. He said, "When can you start?"

I said, "Monday week. I need to give Mr. Bryant a week to find a replacement driver for me. I drive a school bus."

He said, "You drive a school bus?"

I said, "Yes, sir."

He said, "Monday week, go to Ms. Rita when you get here, and she will get you started."

He stood up, and I did also. We shook hands, and I followed him out. As I was leaving, I stopped when I got out of their vision to see if I could hear what he was going to say to Ms. Rita. He told her that that was a good interview. I felt better now that Ms. Rita wasn't in trouble. I left. As I was walking down the railroad tracks toward home, I looked back at the plant, and I could see Mr. Baker looking out of the window. I knew he saw me. When I got home, I went straight up to Papa Badge's house to tell him the news.

This was my first real job. I hitched a ride that day by school bus. I knew some of the bus drivers and had prearranged a drop-off near the plant. I was no more than a hundred yards from the plant. Perfect. I did what Mr. Baker had suggested and got with Ms. Rita. We did some orientation, and she took me to my supervisor, Mr. Johnnie Green.

He was an older white man that seemed to have a nerve problem. His hands trembled a lot. After our introduction, he took me to Mr. Moore. Mr. Moore was a young white man with an athletic build and sandy brown hair. He was a couple inches taller than I. He wasn't but a couple of inches taller, but he was what we call men folk. After we were introduced, he kind of looked at me with this funny look on his face. He looked at me as if he were sizing me up for whatever. Maybe it was because I weighted a little over 125 pounds. Maybe he thought I couldn't do the job. He then took me to the area where we would be working, training on how to doff spinning frames. He went through the spiels on preparation, actual doffing, restarting, retreading, and loading the finished product. We had twelve spinning frames, and the process took about two hours to complete. We went outside for a smoke break. While outside, I noticed that this man was a quiet person. Not one word did he speak during this time. After break, we returned to the working area, and he continued training. At the end of the shift, I began my journey home. Home was a long walk in this bitter cold weather. At midnight, it was brutally cold. Without transportation, I had to get these feet moving. The realization of this hit me in the face. Out of school at three, I had to hitch a ride to work. I had to work eight hours, walk home, get as much sleep as I could, and be up at six to prepare for school. This wasn't going be a cakewalk, no pun intended. The light springtime jacket was not enough to keep me warm. I ran a lot. It was during our break on Friday after a week of not uttering one word all week when Mr. Moore looked at me and said that the supervisor was going to put me on the spinning frames next to his. I would be on my own. I told him that he would be able to handle them. Then he said something that made the hairs on my neck stand up. He said that he had been in and out of prison since he was seventeen. He said, "I've beaten up a lot of guys, and some of them I enjoyed. I have a really bad temper, and when you mix that with drinking, bad things happen. I've been checking around, and everybody says you are a good kid. If I hear that you have gotten into any trouble, I'm going to find you and whoop your ass! I don't want to see you end up in prison or dead." He looked at me, and I knew he wasn't playing. I said that I wouldn't get into any trouble. He smiled for the first time in a week. "OK, let's get back to work," he said. I didn't want to disappoint him or myself for that matter. As time went on, Mr. Moore and I would take smoke breaks together, and his personality and sense of humor came out. He began to loosen up, and I began to enjoy being around him.

After working there for a month, on that day, something beautiful happened. I was in the canteen taking a soda break. Ms. Ford walked in. Ms. Ford was a small-framed white woman around forty, who wore her long hair rolled up on top of her head. This was a strange style. She had a very nice smile and soft brown eyes. I took her to be a loner. She rarely talked to her coworkers. As she was getting the soda from the machine, she said, "You are the young man I see walking down the railroad tracks after work."

I said, "Yes, ma'am."

She said, "Where on earth are you going?"

I said, "Home. I live in Sugar Hill."

"It must be hard walking that far in this weather?"

I replied, "It is. I run a lot." I started laughing. She did also, and I noticed that she had a beautiful smile, the kind that you had to smile back. We sat there enjoying our soda without saying much for the rest of the break. A couple of days went by, and at shift's end, I was going to the door to leave. Ms. Ford stopped me. She said that she would give me a ride if I wanted to. I was not going to turn this down.

I said, "Ms. Ford, people are going to say some bad things about you if they see us together because you are white."

She replied with some anger in her voice, "Yes, I'm white. I really don't care what people think. I don't like the idea that you are out there alone. Something could happen to you, and nobody would know what happened or would care."

"Yes, ma'am. You are right. I never thought about it that way."

She said, "Let's go."

As we were riding home, we made small talk. She mostly did the talking, and I realized that even though she didn't mix and mingle with others, she was very aware of what was going on around her. Like any organization, there was politics or micromanaging the higher-up's decisions. It seemed now that fate or destiny had brought us together. We usually ended up taking breaks and lunch around the same time. I really liked being around her even though she was much older. I always liked being around older people because that was whom you learn the most from. Our relationship had really started to take off. I looked forward to seeing her at work. As our relationship was turning into friendship, we began to talk about a lot of different topics. Ms. Ford had a very charismatic personality and a sense of humor that drew you into her world without resistance. She made you feel good without even knowing it. We laughed a lot, and one night, I asked her why she always wore her hair in that way. She said that she wore it that way for protection.

"Protection," I said.

"Yes," she responded. "It's long as you can see, and I'm afraid that I might get it caught in one of the machines."

"Makes sense to me," I replied. "Ms. Ford, I was wondering how you looked with it down."

"You want me to take my hair down so you can see what I look like?"

I said, "Yeah, if it's not a problem."

She said OK and began to unravel it. This long hair fell perfectly along her neckline, and she began to fluff it and gave it one of those twirls that only white girls can do. She then cut the inside light on the car for my viewing. She looked absolutely beautiful. I was stunned at just how gorgeous she was. The dark-brown hair matched the soft brown eyes naturally. I said to her that I was just amazed at how beautiful she looked. She smiled and said, "Can I put it back up?"

"Yes, but let me have just one more look," I said. She continued to laugh as she was rolling it back up. As I was getting out of the car, I was still saying, "Just beautiful, just beautiful."

It was in early March when we received the news that this incredibly compassionate woman had passed. It devastated me to the point that I was somehow lost. Coming to work during that time was painful. When I heard the news, I went to the back of the department where no one could see me and I cried like a baby. Sometimes I found myself crying while I was working. My coworkers didn't know why, and I didn't tell them. I was grieving. In my mind, I thought that everything with her was all right. She never said anything about her health being good or bad. She was always positive and upbeat during our ride home. The nights that followed, I would walk home, but the bitter winter weather was not as bad because I was always thinking of Ms. Ford. It took weeks for my grief to get back to normal. I always wondered if I could have done something to prevent this tragedy from happening. Most nights, as I was walking home, I remembered some of the fun times we had and how we made fun of each other playfully. I will always treasure those moments and will never forget. Now that I can look back, I really let her down, and I feel bad that I did. I would have loved to have gone to her funeral if I had transportation. Even though the racial climate was bad, I was afraid of the impact, negatively or positively, my being there would have. I would imagine her lying in a casket with her hair down. As I looked back, I still feel the emptiness that her death caused. See, she showed me true kindness and compassion that no one else would in helping a young man get through some bitter times. I didn't stand up and find out what happened to her or attended her funeral, and in some way, I disrespected her because I wasn't as big a man as she was a woman. This lesson changed my views on life as well as friendships forever. Her death taught me not to give in to the ideas of others like racism and separation but to believe in the ideas in me like commonality and friendship and to allow others to be themselves and to stay true to myself. She gave a young man a chance to understand what Papa Badge said—"If you only love those that love you, you have never loved." What she gave to me will always be appreciated and cherished for the remaining time I walk in this earth. Now when I think of Ms. Ford, I always remember another saying by Papa Badge—"Sometimes God takes people we love away because He knows what's best for them." That being true, however, didn't make it better at the time. Rest in peace, Ms. Ford.

GEORGE FULLER

EVOLUTION

I T WAS THE summer when I finally got my first car—a 1964 canary-yellow Chevrolet Impala. I was so proud that I had reached my goal. I kept this machine clean as the state board of health.

It was during the early part of fall that Papa Badge died. He had cancer and didn't know it. His passing not only rocked me, but the people he had met during this journey of life were also affected, Mama Ma especially. No one loved Papa Badge more than I did, except her. I lost a friend, mentor, and father. Who would I turn to when I needed answers? Who would love me without restrictions or conditions? Who would be there for me? This was and still is the hardest death that I've faced so far as I travel to a destiny that I have no idea where it may end. Our spiritual journey never ends. When I enter the gates of heaven and I meet God and His Son Jesus, I'm certain that Jesus will point me to where Papa Badge is, and I will join him in God's kingdom. Secondly, I want to meet and thank all the angels that watched over me during my tenure here on earth.

Those were the saddest few days of my life. It brought back the memories of Mark and Ms. Ford, both of whom I had a rough time in dealing with their passing. And now this happened. I kept thinking that all the people close to me were passing away, and I didn't understand why. What friend would pass next? I must be a jinx. On the day of Papa Badge's funeral, I sat there and recalled some of the memories I had of Papa Badge. One was when I was getting into girls. I didn't understand why my friends had girlfriends, and I seemed to be missing something. I thought that girls were afraid of me or I wasn't good enough for them. One day, Papa Badge was sitting on the front porch. Out of the blue, I asked him why girls seemed to not like me. He told me to come into the house for a minute. So we walked in, and he took me in front of the mirror that was attached to the dresser. He was looking into the mirror at me and said, "What do you see?"

I replied, "I see me and you." He then tapped on the back of my head. I said, "What?"

He said, "What do you see?"

I again responded with the same answer as before, "Me and you."

He said, "Jim, you are not a good-looking young man."

I said, "Really?" *Is Papa Badge telling me that I'm ugly?* He began to laugh at that moment because he knew what I was thinking. He said that looks didn't always get the girls. He continued on to say that the guys that get the girls are athletes and musicians.

"You are not an athlete," he said. "You need a hook."

I said, "What is a hook?"

He laughed even more as I asked the question. He said a hook is something you do to get a girl's attention.

He said, "Maybe it's the way you talk or the way you walk. Sometimes it's how you look at her. See, women notice these things, and when they do and if they like it, they will give you signs that say they are interested. Sometimes they will approach you. Now there is one girl that I know likes you, but you don't see it because you don't know the signs yet. When you figure out who, come tell me. Another thing, I know you and Marvin practice in the backyard. Musicians and athletes get a lot of female attention, so maybe you might want to put a little more time into music."

Well, I did find the girl that liked me, and when I told Papa Badge, he said I was right and said something that we both laughed at. He said that his boy is becoming a man.

Another one was when I was six or maybe seven. I had a toothache and told Papa Badge about it. He said, "Show me which one." I quickly pointed it out. It was one of my front teeth. He took his index finger and began to push it back and forth, then side to side. He said, "Yep, it's ready to go." Then he called out to Mama Ma, "Ma, bring me some of that sewing thread." I thought of what he was going to do with a sewing thread. I was about to find out. He tied a string to the door handle, cut the thread, and tied it around the base of the tooth in question. Then he opened and closed the door to measure the correct distance from me to the door. Then he said, "Step back a few inches." When I was in the position he wanted, he slammed the door closed. The tooth came out without interruption. There was some pain, but it was out, and then he laughed. That was better than any dentist could do. Then he said, "Jim, put it under your pillow, and the tooth fairy will put some money under your pillow tonight while you're sleeping." I did what he suggested, and the next morning, I woke up with fifty cents. I believe in the tooth fairy, don't you?

As I sat there in church during the funeral, all kinds of memories of us together flooded my mind, like the day I was playing in the woods nearby. I had spotted a large beehive in one of the trees, so I decided to throw a few rocks at it until it came tumbling down. I threw rocks at the beehive as hard as I could, and finally, it fell to the earth. What was amazing was those bees were mad at me for disrupting their sanctuary and started coming at me. I took off running, and I could hear them behind me. I estimated there were at least fifty, and the humming sound said they were gaining ground. By now, I had cleared the wooded area, and I could see Papa Badge sitting on the front porch. I knew that if I got inside the house, I would be safe. I increased my speed, and about the time I was within fifty yards of the house, Papa Badge saw what was going on and went inside the house. When I got to the door, he had locked it. I couldn't get in. I was looking at him through the window, and he had this look that said, *You are not coming in here.* I started to call out his name, begging for him to open the door. He looked at me and said, "You better cover up your head."

I said in a frantic voice, "Let me in! I need to get inside!" That was when the attack began. The bees were attacking me with an entourage of bites. They were relentless with their attack, stinging me from head to toe. After the barrage of bites ceased and the coast was clear, Papa Badge opened the door, laughing out of his mind.

He said, "Jim, you won't be messing around with any beehives no time soon, will you?" I was so mad at him for leaving me out to dry. I didn't respond. Then he called Mama Ma to bring him some alcohol, which she did immediately. Then he told me to undress from head to toe. When I finished, he lay down on the porch facedown. Then he began to rub that alcohol all over my back and legs. This was more painful than the bites. Then he did the front side. Pulling the stingers out was just an added bonus. It was not a fun day for me, but Papa Badge loved every minute of it. I used the memories of Papa Badge to help with my grief, but it didn't take away the pain or loneliness I felt.

After Papa Badge's death, Mama Ma began to have a series of strokes. We had gotten close, and she would always talk about Papa Badge. These strokes affected the right side of her body, and she couldn't use the arm at all. Then her mind began to decline along with her speech. It got to the point where we couldn't provide or give her the attention she needed medically. Mother decided to put her in a nursing home. She passed away within six months of Papa Badge's passing, and again, I was devastated. Within a year and a half, I had lost four people that I admired. I was so devastated I began to listen to the bad angels. They were telling me to take a drink. These bad angels said, "It will make you feel better. Here, smoke a little weed." "Try some of these drugs." "Oh, this cocaine is the newest and the greatest thing out." "Don't forget the girls. Get many of them as you can because you have got to get as many notches on your belt as you can." "Life is a party, and you may as well dance your butt off." I did everything these bad angels said, and before I realized it, I was high all the time. I couldn't wait to get high. It just appeared to take away the loneliness I was going through. It wasn't, and I was just fooling myself. I was completely out of control and didn't care who I hurt as long as I was getting what I wanted—sex and drugs. They just went together. Sometimes I would find myself in hotel rooms and didn't have a clue as to how I got there. I was so selfish that if your wife was good-looking, I would go after her, and a lot of times, I succeeded without any regard to what impact it had on their marriage. I was out of control. It was all about me.

Some of my friends were telling me about this company that was hiring. They paid more money than what I was making, so I said I'll give it a shot because the price of sex and drugs had gone up, and I want to stay in the game. I mean, I had been at this company for a couple of years, and it was time for a change. I got hired on second shift in the department called the dyehouse. They trained me for a week on the first shift, and then I moved to my regular shift. My job responsibility was to weigh the dyestuffs needed and place the content in a bucket for the drug men to mix and transfer down to the dyehouse kettles, where the fabric would be dyed into the proper colors. I worked with three older gentlemen: Mr. Anthony Robinson, Mr. Timothy Davis, and Mr. Larry Washington Taylor. Mr. Robinson I knew from Sugar Hill days. He was maybe in his fifties. He knew Papa Badge well and would speak about him occasionally after we were introduced. A big man with curly hair and a dry sense of humor but carried himself in a respectable manner that required you give him the same, Mr. Robinson vouched for me to get this job. I didn't know at the time, but a bell should have went off when I saw him smiling on my first day. Mr. Timothy Davis was a small man not much larger than I but carried himself like Mr. Robinson. Mr. Davis was a neat, stylish person and had a charismatic personality. Mr. Taylor was like Mr. Robinson in size. Both had short curly hair, and Mr. Taylor was a couple of shades lighter than Mr. Robinson was. Mr. Robinson was the life of the party. He would have us laughing all night. He also couched the others about me. We all had a great time working together, and for some reason, they tutored me on the operation like a father would do a son.

On my first day on the shift, we were all sitting around the workstation, and the conversation about this young man started. Mr. Davis said to Mr. Robinson, "Timothy, do you want to tell George about Daniel Jordan?"

Mr. Robinson said, "No, Tim, you tell him."

I said, "Tell me what?" Then Tim started to say that Daniel was a redneck white fellow who comes up here around six o'clock every day to weigh dyes for his department.

He said, "He's ex-marine—from South Carolina and mean as a snake. Cusses like a sailor and didn't care nothing about no one or anything. He don't like us black folks a bit. We try to stay away from him. Nobody likes him because not only is he mean but arrogant to boot. He's loud and has a nasty attitude. Even his supervisor is scared of him. He just soon as fight you as to look at you. When he comes up here, don't say anything to him."

At around six o'clock, I could hear James coming up the stairs. Like Mr. Tim said, he was cussing some kind of bad about something that had occurred in their department. He was not alone. He and the other person went into the room, and about that time, an order came up for me to weigh. So I went into the weight room where these two people were. They looked up when I entered the room and I said to them, "Hi, I'm George." I extended my hand for a handshake, and Daniel seemed startled for a moment and then we shook hands. He then introduced the other guy, who also shook my hand. I smiled and turned to the other scale to finish the order. The room remained silent after that. I completed the task and went outside to where the guys were looking at me as they were asking me what happened. Daniel Jordan was white, like they said, with a full beard. He was probably around the same age as me but weighed more with a little beer belly. We were the same height. He had those piercing eyes that said something like, *Are you for real?* or *I don't believe you for one minute.* He was a rugged kind of fellow, and when he spoke, he gave it to you straight and didn't care if you liked it. He was my kind of person—no sugarcoating or trying to be politically correct. This was how I saw it, so I got over it. As the weeks went by, we began to exchange our opinions on a lot of topics. We often agreed, but when we didn't, we didn't take it personally. I showed him a lot of respect, and he did the same. He didn't cuss like he used to around me for some reason, and I didn't either.

One night, he said that he and a coworker were going up to the local pizzeria after work and wanted to know if I wanted to come. I said, "Yes. I'll meet you there." When I told the guys, I got all kinds of reactions like, "Don't do it. It's a setup. They are going to do something that's going to hurt you. Don't trust him or them." I could understand their fears. This town was racist. I knew that. I didn't feel like I was in danger or that he would do something to hurt me. I just didn't. There was not a lot of race mixing in this town, and I wasn't trying to be a pioneer in race relation either. I was trying to be what I was shown to by Ms. Ford in that I would not let other people's view of the world affect me. You do what your mind and heart dictate and be true to yourself.

When I arrived at the pizzeria, it was packed this Friday night, and this was one of the more popular places in town. I walked in and immediately spotted James and the other coworker. To my surprise, Daniel's wife and daughter were there. We greeted one another with a handshake, and afterward, he introduced me to the family along with a friend, Paul. His wife was from South Carolina also. Jessie Burns was a local guy and was working in the quality lab at the plant. We were getting a lot of attention in the form of stares, but no one said anything. For some strange reason, I felt comfortable in this setting even though it was different. The night went along very well, and when I left, I came away with a new respect for Daniel, Jessie, and of course, myself. We all bonded that night, and even though I had just met Jessie, he seemed down-to-earth and real.

When I got to work the next day, the guys began to question me about the evening. More than that, they were glad to see me alive. They began to look at Daniel differently too. They knew that he didn't let anything happen to me, and for that, he earned their respect. They began to talk to him when he came upstairs. He would always return the favor. We all began to talk to one another, and I knew Daniel liked the attention he was getting when he was upstairs. After that night, we began to really jell and would often take a smoke break together before we headed home.

On this night, we were in the parking lot, and Daniel said some things that really blew me away. He began to tell me about his experiences in Vietnam. He said that one night, they got hit by Charlie (Viet Cong), and they were hitting them with firepower that they couldn't keep up with. They had radioed for backup and were waiting for air support to get them out of this jam. He said that a lot of soldiers were getting killed, and with the amount of firepower they were hit with, all he and the others could do was to lie on the dead soldiers' bodies to stop the amount of hits they were taking even though they were already dead. He said that that night he realized what it meant to lay your life down for someone else. The air support came and pushed the Viet Cong back into the bush, and as he rolled off the dead body, he was so proud to be an American. As he continued to talk, I came to the conclusion that he needed to talk about these experiences because he had been carrying them around for a long time. I felt privileged for him to express these valuable lessons with me, and I encouraged him to tell me more. He did. He opened up like a spring flower in bloom. He said as he continued to talk that I reminded him of a young soldier he met in 'Nam. He said this young guy always wanted to lead the platoon when they were in the bush. On this particular day, he had pleaded with Daniel to let him do it. Daniel said that he was reluctant at first to do so, but the young man's persistence overrode his judgment, and he gave in. The point man's responsibility is to be in front of the platoon. He leads the other soldiers to a destination given by the commanding officer. He tries to spot enemy aggressors and warns the platoon on location and number of soldiers and, of course, firepower. As they were walking up this trail, they got hit by enemy fire, and all hell broke loose. After the encounter, Daniel said he was looking for the young soldier to compliment him on what a good job he had done. When he found him, he turned him over, and immediately he knew he was killed. He said, "Man, I blamed myself for his death. If I had stuck by my gut instincts, he would be alive." As they prepared the young soldier's body to be evacuated to headquarters for the long flight home, he knew that he would never see this young soldier again. Even though that might be true, the decision he made would haunt him forever.

I said, "Daniel, I see you limping when you walk. What caused that?"

He said that a few days after the young soldier was killed, they were back in the bush again. This time, however, he was the point man. As he was leading the platoon, he stepped on something, and when he heard a clicking sound, he knew what it was—a mine. He said that he also knew that when he stepped off, it would explode and that would be the end for him. He threw up his hand to alert the platoon as to what was happening. He told them about the situation and ordered them to keep walking and to not look back. He also said that as each soldier passed by, they shook his hand to say farewell. He said that he asked God to forgive him for the decision he made about the young soldier. When they got out of sight, he jumped off the mine. When he came to, he was in the infirmary. He realized that the platoon came back and rescued him and took him to safety. He said that he was told that he would be transferred to Paris Island for recovery. That was where he met his wife. He said that the doctors told him he was lucky that he only lost half of his left foot. It wasn't luck. It was God's grace and mercy that saved him. He also told me that he was going to the quality lab at the beginning of the month. That was a promotion. Once you got into the lab, it was a training prerequisite for being a manufacturing supervisor. Then he said this: "Once I'm in, I'll get you in. You can count on it. You, too, would make a fine supervisor." I thanked him for the compliment, and we both laughed and went home.

One day, my supervisor Sam Worthy called me in the office. He said that I have an interview in the quality lab with Mr. Bush. He was the manager of the department. It was at four o'clock. It was now three forty-five. In the drug room, we wore raggedy old clothing because we handle different colorants and chemicals such as acids that would do bodily damage if not handled properly. What I was saying was that the clothing I was wearing wasn't what you would want to wear to an interview. Not only that, my hair was in plaits because that was the style then. When I walked in for the interview, I apologized for my appearance. Mr. Bush began to laugh because he knew that I would be dressed that way. He said it was not the clothing that he was interviewing but me. The interview went well, and I was hired for the position. On the way back to the department, I kept thinking about Daniel and how he looked after me and did what he said. Over the next fifteen years, our friendship had been one that most people would envy. Two people from different cultures and backgrounds had developed a friendship that most people would envy because it was built on trust and respect. Unfortunately, Daniel passed away around 1995 from a massive heart attack. I was living out of town at the time, and when I moved back in 1997, that was when I found out. I was trying to relocate some of the friends I had made before leaving. Thank you, Daniel, for all you have given, but most importantly, thank you for being who you are.

Once I got into the lab, I knew that my drug issue had to come to an end. This job meant that people would be watching me closely in and out of the plant. I didn't want them to know that I was a druggie. I kept it hidden, and just a handful knew of my problem. I knew, and that was what was important, and I had to find the answer on how to quit. Sometimes when you are looking for something, it finds you, not the other way around.

It was Friday after work, and all I could think of was getting high. I did. One thing about being high was you sometimes have a real disconnect with your compassionate side. You become I oriented, and no one's feelings seem to matter but yours. I took off uptown to a local Quik Mart convenience store. This was where I purchased my eight-track tapes. When I entered the store, there were a few people inside. When I got to the music section, I heard this commotion at the end of one of the aisles. As I turned around to see what was going on, around the corner came none other than Brian Mayo. Brian had been paralyzed from the waist down after a tree-cutting accident that involved a power saw. I was told that he was cutting a tree with a power saw and lost his balance, and the saw fell over his head and ended up severely cutting his spinal cord. That was when the bad angel told me to ask him about how he knew I was on fire in the house that day. He was supposed to be in school. So I just pimped on over to where he was. I knew that he knew that I was high. So I approached him in a cool manner and asked the question. He just looked at me for a second, and then he said that God told him to go to Papa Badge's house, and that was when he saw that I was on fire. I instantly came crashing down from my high and realized that I was so insensitive to the condition he was in and what he had to deal with in regard to his injury. Plus I was disrespectful. I was so humiliated by my behavior I ran out of the store. I went home and went into my room without turning the lights on. I started to cry, thinking that this young man saved my life. Now fate had really given him a bad blow and left him crippled. I couldn't believe I had the audacity to say what I did. That was so inconsiderate, so cold. I had never been so ashamed of my actions as I was on that day. I continued to cry. I couldn't go to sleep. All I could do was cry. I knew I was in trouble. I desperately needed help. I had been crying for hours. I said to myself, "God, what can I do?"

Later on that evening, this feeling of warmth surrounded me. I had this feeling before but didn't quite understood it. I felt again the relaxation that came with it, and I knew that something was going to happen. That same voice I heard when Mark and I were talking said, "You can do better." Then the feeling disappeared along with the voice. I made a vow to not do drugs again that night. For the remainder of the weekend, I stayed in my room. I also knew that when I left this room, I would not be the same person that entered. Brian Mayo had saved me for the third time in less than fifteen years, and I didn't have the courage to thank him. There was only shame. I couldn't face him. I was so ashamed. I know now that God had put earthly angels here for me despite my flaws. Now that I can look back, I can see the wonders of His grace. He didn't give up on me even though I was lost. He just kept sending angels to put me on the right path. He gave me love when I didn't believe nobody loved me. I'm so thankful for His grace, for looking over a sinner like me. He continued to bless me, and I don't know why. Every time I think that the world is against me, He shows up to remove all doubts and reconfirms His love for me, little old me. Now that I'm recalling my earthly angels, Brian was my angel for the third time. If my mind was in the right place, then maybe things would have been different then, but would it have been different now? You get the answers when He's ready for you to do His will. Do you really think God does all these things for you without any expectations from you? He simply asks that you glorify His name. It's not hard to give a shout-out to Him in just regular conversation, is it?

PRAYER

WHAT IS A prayer? To me, a prayer is a tool that allows you to communicate directly to God. A prayer is meant to strengthen your personal relationship with the Master. When I go into my sanctuary, I go in just like I came into the world. To me, this indicates humility and respect. Also, I don't ask for items that will increase my material worth, like cars, money, or fancy homes. What I ask for are things like compassion and understanding of the things that I cannot change. I center on love of country, understanding of the many issues that have an impact on others, growth in faith, and the need for Him in my life. When I'm at the closing of my prayer, I thank Him for the many blessings that He has given me when I was spiritually dead. One of the greatest lessons I've learned during this journey was once you ask Him to come into you, your spiritual journey will never end. God will just amaze you with His love.

For a long time, I did what all men did as young men do—playing the field. Then one day, I realized that this game was all it was—a game. So I decided to get a part-time job to keep myself busy and out of trouble. I had cleaned up my act and hadn't used any drugs in eight years and counting. I was afraid that if I didn't play music I would do something until the opportunity presents itself. I landed a part-time gig at a local gas station pumping gas and servicing customer needs. My hours were from 5:00 p.m. to eleven. Back then, there were no self-service stations. You drive in, tell the attendant what kind and how much, and pay afterward.

One weekend, I was thinking about how I was going to change my attitude or perception about women. Then it dawned on me to pray about it. I also remembered what Papa Badge had said about prayer. He said that God already knows what you are going to say well before you say it. However, if you want something other than fancy clothes, a mansion, a high-dollar car, or money, then humble yourself to Him. What he continued to say was when you humble yourself, you are showing and giving Him respect. To do that, you have to disrobe and go into your sanctuary. A sanctuary can be anywhere you feel comfortable and private. I chose the bathroom. I did what Papa Badge said, and when I went into my sanctuary, I said this: "Father, I know you know the kind of man I am. What I really need is to change my ways. To meet a woman that will show me how to love because the way I'm going is the wrong way. I'm just using them for sex, lying, giving them a false intention, and more than that, somehow degrading their self-esteem. I don't want to continue this way. Thank you for hearing my prayer." I got up from my knees and went to bed. A couple of weeks went by, and one night, this car pulled in, and she requested two dollars of gas. She paid me with a two-dollar check. Once I finished, she smiled and drove away. Later on that night, my mind was trying to recall where I had seen this truly lovely lady. It was at work. We passed each other in the aisle, and we greeted and smiled at each other. She had a beautiful smile. I did a one-eighty degree turn to see what she looked like from behind. That was something I never did, but for some reason, I broke tradition. It was worth it too. She had a very slim body that moved in a sensuous and sexy way. She was bad.

Two days later, she came by and again wrote another two-dollar check. She smiled and left. That night at closing, I was doing the tabulation for monies made when the check came up. I looked at it. The name on it was Vivian C. Winstead. Then I saw her phone number, and that was when it hit me. She wanted me to call her. She was interested. I didn't know. I mean, this woman had just lost her husband about a year ago. I couldn't play games with her. She was, in my mind, vulnerable, and to do something like that to her when she needed much more would be taking advantage of her. That was what I was trying to put behind me. I mean, she was going through a lot, dealing with the passing of a loved one. If I proceed, I would have to be straight with her. She needed someone special to help her get through these hard times. I finished the money count, cut the lights out, and went home. I didn't think about the young lady after that night.

On July 5, 1985, the first lady came in with some of her friends. When I approached her car, the tone in her voice was different. She spoke to me in a degrading manner that I didn't expect, which totally caught me off guard. She said, "Put the gas in. You should know by now. If you can remember back three days ago." Her friends just laughed. I put the gas in, and when I approached her for the money, she started to count out loud the amount. She said this in a slow voice, and the tone indicated that I wasn't the sharpest tack in the drawer. The car was filled with laughter. She lingered on with this charade until she had given me all that was required. Then she rolled her eyes at me in disapproval. During this ordeal, I maintained my professionalism. But I was somewhat hurt.

By then, cars were coming into the lot by the dozen, it seemed. I was backed up. The first car in was a carful of Mexicans, six to be exact. The driver said, "Five dollars of regular." Then the others got out and watched as I put the gas in. Why? Maybe they were high. I didn't understand the need for this. They were holding me up. Then they started asking questions in Spanish, which I didn't understand. I was trying to get to the other customers as quickly and efficiently as I could, and they were standing in my way, preventing me from doing so. I finally told the driver to get in the car and park in an area that I designated by hand gesture and I would answer their questions after I caught up. He got in the car and headed to the area, and the rest of them were walking behind the car speaking in Spanish. When I caught up, I went over to answer their questions, but the language barrier was beyond my comprehension. Nothing was solved, and they left mad because I didn't understand them. Working for the public has its rewards, but tonight was not going to be one. About an hour later, this little red Escort pulled in. I was so down by all the negative things going on around me that day.

When I got to her car, I said, "This has been one of the worst days you can imagine. It seems that my customers are saying things that are insulting, degrading, or just flat-out mean. What I really need is for you to just give me a smile." I truly believed that would make me feel so much better. She did. It was far more beautiful than I expected. I felt so good, and it was so real that I told her that I would get off at eleven. I said, "If you want to talk or something, it would be nice."

She said, "OK. I'll come around eleven, and we can go down to my mom's house." Good. She left. It was about ten forty-five when she pulled into the parking lot. At eleven, I closed up shop, and away we went. To my surprise, we were neighbors. Small world. As we sat in the car at her mother's yard, we talked about everything. She was direct and straightforward in her demeanor. We asked questions about each other, and we connected because it was so real in the answers we gave. There was no sugar coating anything. I was impressed because I had finally met someone who was real and would not be influenced by the world but just travel the road she had chosen.

About an hour or two in the conversation, something beautiful happened. As she continued to talk, her voice was drifting away, but I could hear her. This incredible feeling came into me, and suddenly this voice calmly said, "She's the one." I knew that God had answered my prayer. This would be the one God had chosen, the one I would marry. There was never a doubt in my mind. The next day, we got together, and it was on from then to now. I had never been happier in my life. As our relationship began to blossom, there was trust and respect that I found enjoyable. So when she asked me if I would go out to her late husband's grave with her, I didn't hesitate to say yes. It would mark the first year of his homecoming. We went out and cleaned his grave and placed a flower on it. I felt so proud to do so. I knew him through school. We were not like buddies, but he always spoke and would say something positive about whatever the subject was. For me, it was like visiting an old friend. After we did what was needed at the grave site, she took me to visit her ex-mother-in-law. Again, I had no issues with that either. They were a part of her life for a long time, and why shouldn't it continue? When we arrived at her ex-mother-in-law's home, she welcomed me in. We dated heavily for a couple of years and moved to Durham, North Carolina. Life was good.

There will always be times when prayer is the only way to go. In the spring of 1990, I was working two jobs to maintain an income that would put us over the top financially. For about a month, there was something strange going on with my wife. She seemed distant and aloof. Then she began to come home late. On Memorial Day weekend, I questioned her about her behavior. The response I got was not satisfactory. I was thinking that she was running around. What happened next really didn't surprise me. I became violent, physically violent, that she ran out of the house to protect herself. I didn't know how far I would have gone, but I knew that I was going to hurt her. I didn't care about anything but laying down some pain. I wanted to hurt her badly. I had lost it. I had never been so mad. When she left, I went to her job and created a domestic scene. I later returned home. I knew she wouldn't return and the marriage was over. The next day, I had finally calmed down and reflected on what had happened. I realized that I was out of control but, more importantly, ashamed of my behavior. I needed help. I disrobed and went into my sanctuary and began to pray. I asked God to remove the anger in me. I knew that she wouldn't come back, and I really couldn't blame her. I didn't want to be seen as being abusive to anyone, especially a woman.

Two days had gone by, and that morning, there was a knock on the door. When I answered, it was a deputy sheriff. He asked me to verify who I was, and he stated why he was there. I did what he asked. He stood there for moment then asked if he could come in. Yes was my response. We sat down on the sofa, and he began to explain what the procedure was in my situation. Then he took another look at me and said that he was pretty good at reading people. He said that his instincts told him I was not a bad person and I just made a mistake. He went on to tell me about what he would do in the same situation. He went on to say that he would not handcuff me or put me in the back seat like a common criminal. I took his advice, and off to jail we went. I asked him if he could follow me to the bedroom where my checkbook was. He did. We left, and he explained what would happen once we arrived at the magistrate office.

I was released after posting bail. I had to walk home because cabs didn't take checks. We had a hearing in some twenty days. At the hearing, my wife testified to what had happened. When this beautiful woman began to cry, I knew it was over. The judge threw me out of the house that day. Continuing with the guidelines that came with a restraining order, I had nowhere to go. I slept in my car. At work, I told my friend from Saudi Arabia about my situation, and he allowed me to use the bathroom at a local gas station. Sleeping in a car was no good day at the park. Mosquito bites were all over my body, and one of my coworkers asked me what was going on. I told him, and he suggested that I come and live with him and another coworker. It sounded good to me. My friend from the Middle East told me that he was going back home in October to work on the shipping dock. He went on to say that I would make three to four times what I was currently making. He said that he would show me the ropes as far as passports, paperwork, and all the requirements of being in a foreign country. I agreed to go. My life here sucked, and this would be me starting over. Over the next couple of months, I worked my two jobs and had accumulated a large sum of money. One night, I decided to call my wife even though I knew I was going against the restraining order. I just had to tell her something. I rode around until I spotted a pay phone. After a couple of rings, she finally answered. I said that when I left, I had nothing—no money and no place to live in. I said, "I just want you to know that I'm back on my feet, and you can kiss my butt." I hung up. It felt good to say that even though it was very immature.

After a couple of months, we got my passport, and all requirements had been met. We were excited about the news. Things were getting better. September rolled around. My coworker's apartment was in the poorest parts of town. High crime was the norm. Nobody messed with me. It might be because I worked two jobs, and they were asleep when I got off and when I left for my first job. In September, I was in bed that Sunday watching a football game when I heard a knock on the door. It couldn't be for me because no one knew I was living here. After a few seconds, my roommate Joe came into the room. He said, "Fuller, the most beautiful woman I've ever seen is out there, and she wants to talk to you." Joe was the type who was a practical joker. He liked to keep things lively. I knew this was a prank, so I decided to play along with it. I got up and went to the door. When I opened it, it was Puddin, my wife. I got so weak in the knees that I thought I would fall down.

I was completely stunned. She said that she wanted to talk and asked if we could go somewhere. I told her there was a park nearby. When we arrived, we found a spot where we could be alone. As we sat there on the ground, she began to tell me what she was going through. She had visited her doctor, and she told her that she was in the first stage of menopause. I didn't know anything about this topic but knew it was something women go through. She went on to tell me her fears. I listened. I told her that I was going to Saudi Arabia in a couple of weeks, that I would get a new start. I really had to deal with the anger issues I had. I didn't trust myself being around women with the issues I had. I got up to leave. I was waiting for her to get up, but she just sat there weeping. She said that she was not afraid that I would do what I did. She went on to say that if I was that aware of that, then knowing me, I wouldn't let that happen again.

She continued on to say that her life was much better with me. I asked her if she really trusted me. She said, "Yes. Before, I couldn't get the word out of my mouth." I thought about it for a minute and decided that she was whom I wanted to be with. So I walked back to where she was sitting and said, "Let's go home." We did.

The next day, I was traveling to my second job when I noticed that there were a lot of medical offices in the area. I pulled in and went inside. The receptionist asked if she could be of help to me. I said, "My wife is going through menopause, and I need someone to tell me what I need to know that will make her life better." She went to the back, and this doctor appeared. She broke things down from every possible angle, making sure that I was grasping all the information given. I retained the info. When I turned around to leave, people began to clap. That was when I realized that I was in a gynecologist's office.

Once we got on track, I asked her how she knew where I lived. She said she didn't know. I knew that nobody followed me. That was something I was sure of. I believed that God had a hand in it. It's been over twenty-five years, and I never raised my hands in anger toward anyone. Prayer is power.

It was in early spring of 2002 when I became restless. My work schedule had changed, and I had a lot of free time on my hands. I needed a hobby to keep me busy and engaged. So I decided to try writing, since this was something I always wanted to try. What would I write about? Love? We had moved from Durham to Roxboro to be closer to our parents. My wife is a full-blooded Native, and we began to get involved in her history. We started out with workshops in the winter, and when spring arrived, we moved outdoors. What does one do outdoors? We began to attend what some call powwows. The correct term is simply a gathering. On this particular weekend in May, we attended a local gathering. As the gathering was coming to a close, we were asked to go to a particular spot for prayer, which we agreed to. The tribe's minister had set up the area with the proper ointment needed for the moment. Our role was to receive the ointments and place it in the circle and say a prayer afterward. When my turn came, I approached the circle and violently threw the sage into the circle. I stepped back in line and said no prayer. All the attendants were shocked at my behavior and attitude. I could see the disappointment in my wife. Everybody was disappointed in me. When we got to my car, my wife let me know how disappointed she was in me. I couldn't explain it either. I kept asking myself, Why? The answer never came.

It was in October of the same year when my friend and I were approached by an HR rep at work. She explained to us that she wanted someone outside of management to say a prayer at the annual service banquet. We both declined. After a few moments, I gave in and agreed to do it. On the drive home, I kept thinking about why I volunteered and what I was going to say. Most of the time, when I work on my off day, I usually take a little nap. As I lay in bed, the thought about what I was going to say was hanging heavily on my mind. Suddenly, this voice said, "Get up and write these words." I leaped out of bed, found a paper and pen, and sat down on the edge of the bed. This voice told me what to write, and I followed the command given without looking at the paper. I was just writing. It was as if I were under a spell, but a beautiful one. When I finished, I walked down the hallway to the living room, where my wife was watching TV. I gave her the paper where I had written the words that God had given me. She took a glance and returned to watching TV. She played me off. I looked at the paper and decided that I would type it up, learn it, and say it at the upcoming event. I faithfully practiced this prayer daily until the day of the event. Finally, the moment arrived. When the emcee introduced me to say the prayer, something beautiful happened. When I received the mic, this incredible warmth surrounded me. I noticed that as I began to say the prayer, I couldn't hear myself talk. I continued to speak, but I was just moving my mouth. I knew that I was saying the prayer. When I finished and sat down at the table assigned to me, people began to congratulate me and said what an outstanding job I had done. The plant manager's wife topped it all off when she said it was the best prayer she had ever heard. When the event was over, a lot of people came over to congratulate me. Since that night, my coworkers looked at me differently—respectfully.

The following year, we returned to the site of my last debacle. This time, I decided to say the prayer that God had given me. When called on, I took a couple of steps toward the circle, and immediately the Holy Spirit engaged me and I said the prayer like I owned it. Afterward, I noticed tears were meeting under my chin. I returned to my position in the circle. My friends were just looking at me with this I-can't-believe look. They were simply blown away. My wife was too. I realized that when God gives you something to do or say, He sends the Holy Spirit to help you through the moment.

Another moment that increased my belief system started in winter of 2012. I began to have headaches. At first, I didn't pay much attention to them. As they increased, I just took over-the-counter products, and that was the end of that—or so I thought. They came back. Now I was getting worried, so I immediately went to my personal doctor. There was not much he could do. Another year went by. My personal doctor suggested that I go see a neurologist. I did. After a consultation with the neurologist, nothing was prescribed, and the headaches continued. Another year went by with the headaches continuing. In 2014, the headaches intensified. On the first of January, I received the news that my childhood friend Marvin had passed. Growing up together from as far back as I can remember, there wasn't a day that we didn't play. As we grew older, we practiced playing our favorite instrument. When we became teenagers, he taught me how to drive. After that, we became adults and went in the direction life had given us. After I went through drug rehab and tried to get my life back on track, he stepped in and invited me to join his quartet. He knew that I was not in the class he was. To him, we were in the backyard practicing again. We really missed hanging out together. Starting out, I made a lot of mistakes. He never talked down to me for my errors but suggested that we set up a weekly schedule to practice. We did. We practiced five nights a week and played with the group on Sundays. He was responsible for the success I had as a musician. His death really touched me in a variety of ways. The most was that I was the last of our childhood group to remain alive. What kept going through my mind was, Why me? I was the last one standing, and there were no answers. Why me? What I did notice was that the headaches continued. They were lasting longer, and the over-the-counter meds weren't working. I continued to think about Marvin regularly. I don't know if that caused my situation to escalate, but it didn't help.

Even today, there are situations that occur that remind me of him, especially when I'm listening to music. I know that when I think of Marvin, I realize that he was the lucky one, and I'm grateful for that.

It was during Thanksgiving when these headaches were beginning to intensify at a level that was concerning, to say the least. The neurologist didn't seem to care, or he just didn't take the time needed to resolve the issue.

By 2015, the headaches had turn into migraines then migraines turned into seizures. Finally, after complaining, the neurologist called me for a series of tests. They did an MRI, a CAT scan, blood work, and a procedure called spinal tap. I was told to return when they set up an appointment to go over the test results. They did call to discuss the results. Two days prior to that appointment, I noticed that my right eyelid was beginning to close. The migraines had gotten so bad that I was put on long-term disability at work. I couldn't perform a simple task. There was loss of balance and loss of sight. Plus when you are having migraines that severe, the last thing you need is noise. On the day of my appointment, the PA examined me and began to tell me that the results were inconclusive and that the tests would have to be redone because some of the samples were not retained. As for my right eyelid closing, I would have to set up another appointment. I got mad and frustrated and left the facility. I had been coming there for two-plus years, and I was no better off than when I started. When I returned home, I called my doctor to recommend another neurologist. Over the next two days, the right eyelid closed even more.

On July 4, it closed completely. I ran off to the local hospital. There they performed a CAT scan. In the meantime, I decided to go outside for a smoke. I needed to relax. My buddy showed up and joined me for the treat. We went outside and began to burn one. My friend loved to talk. As he was talking, I noticed that his voice was drifting away, but I could still understand what he was saying. Suddenly, this warm but cool breeze surrounded me, and everything became quiet. Then I heard this voice say, "I'm here." Then as quickly as this breeze came, it left. My wife called out to me to return because the doctor was ready to discuss what the tests revealed.

When I entered the room and the doctor looked at me, he said, "You are having a brain aneurysm, and the last thing you need is to be smoking." I looked at my wife, then at my buddy and others in the room. They had that expression that said, *He is going to die tonight.* The doctor said that he was affiliated with a local hospital in Durham. He works there as a neurologist and had set up transportation and had also arranged for surgery when I arrive. Then he said, "Sit over there and don't move." He was mad at me for smoking. Transportation arrived shortly, and we were on our way. As I sat there, my mind went back to the parking lot and what had happened. God had spoken to me, and I knew that I wasn't going to die this night even though everybody thought I would. God came to reassure me of that.

Transportation arrived shortly, and we were off to our destination. The EMS personnel that was assigned to me began to ask medical questions. What was the reason I was being transported? When I told her that I was having a brain aneurysm, gloom filled out her face. She immediately began to make me as comfortable as possible, making sure I was warm enough. She began to pat me, and I told her, "I know you are afraid that I'm going to die, but relax, it's not going to happen tonight." She just looked at me without saying a word. I could see she was getting emotional, so I didn't press the issue. Again, my mind kept thinking about that incredible, amazing moment in the parking lot. For some reason, I couldn't tell them that the Holy Spirit appeared in the form of a warm, cool breeze to prepare me for the arrival of my Father, my God, to speak to me. He was there to reassure me that I would be all right, and more importantly, I believe Him. Since that night, I've recovered well. My right eyelid has opened, and my vision is much better. I haven't had a headache or migraine since. I've also had a heart bypass surgery, and I'm presently in rehab. When this book is complete, I will have completed the covenant that I made to God. If you are reading this book, you know that my covenant is fulfilled.

SPECIAL EARTHLY ANGEL

A LOT OF times, God, in His wisdom and grace, designates earthly angels in our lives to carry out His agenda. These earthly angels may lie dormant for years until the time arrives for them to perform His task. This is true in my case.

In the year 2000, my work schedule changed, and I ended up with a lot of free time on my hands. To fill the void, I decided to give writing a try. It was just something I always wanted to do. One day, I was sitting in front of my computer getting ready to play some solitaire. At that time, my mind was on a friend that was going through some tough times. Suddenly, a voice said, "Write this." I did, and the voice was patient because I was no speed demon on the keyboard. Afterward, I knew that this was for the person I was thinking about. I then gave this message to him. The funny thing is, I can't remember what I wrote some seventeen years later. After thinking about this, I came to the conclusion that God had designated me to do this task. More words came, and I was so proud to carry out His mission. I found myself doing more, and the reaction I got from the recipients was truly wonderful. Sometimes, when I was around those I had given the letters or poems to, they and their relatives would give me high praise for what I had done. I simply told them that I was the messenger—a blessing that God had planned for me to do. Since I was given this responsibility, I became motivated and thought it would be a good idea if I got into the Word.

I started reading the Bible. At first, it seemed complicated to understand what the meaning was. I became frustrated. It dawned on me that I needed someone who had the knowledge and wisdom to help me. That was when I went to this special lady. She was beautiful in every way. She had the perfect demeanor, an aura that made one feel automatically attracted to her. I began to tell her about the special gift I was given and the satisfaction I felt delivering these messages to those that God had given me. She reminded me that God has a purpose for all of us. She reminded me to embrace it. As our conversations grew, I began to explain to her that reading the Bible can be confusing, and that frustrated me. She simply replied that if I needed help, she would be there to help me along the way. I continued to read the Bible, and when we saw each other, I would point out the phrases or scriptures I didn't understand. She would break it down to where I did, and she told me how to apply them to everyday life. It was so beautiful to listen her, and I could see the joy in her face when she spoke about God. That love for God transferred into me. Sometimes during our discussions, it was like she knew what my next question was and answered before I asked. That was so amazing to me. I would ask some really dumb questions, and she never made fun of me or made me feel inadequate for asking. This interaction made me feel so good, knowing that I had someone to talk to. She reminded me of Papa Badge. We began to spend more time together, and it was like going to church but only doing the week. We began to attend church services together, and afterward we went out to lunch. We would always discuss what was said during the sermon. What it meant was I was growing spiritually. I was so happy. This was a special time for me. I began to affectionately call her girlfriend. She was the second woman I attended church services with. Our relationship just ballooned afterward. I found myself yearning to be around her because of the knowledge and wisdom she was giving me. I was learning far more than I expected. It took a few years, but God gave me the opportunity to look back and identify those who played a major role in my development to becoming a better Christian. I came to the conclusion that my special angel had done more than listen to me. She had become my spiritual adviser, mentor, and friend. She reconnected me to God at a much higher level than I was before. She set me up without me knowing it to understand the love God has for me and all others. She did this without telling me how to do it but allowed me to figure it out on my own. She knew I would follow the path she provided because she was wiser than most. Wisdom is one of God's blessings, and He only gives it to those that He has selected. I'm glad He chose her to help me understand and appreciate His love. The conversations we shared are still ingrained in my mind and my heart. Those lessons will live a lifetime in me, and if I'm lucky, I can give it back to someone who was just like me.

GEORGE FULLER

AUTOBIOGRAPHY

I F YOU HAD approached me ten years ago and told me I would write a book, I would have laughed in your face. I'm not laughing now. The purpose of me doing this is I have had the honor to see those of blessings I've been given. I'm just a common man with little ambition to take on such an enormous endeavor. I had no plans to reach for such a lofty goal. That wasn't my plan. God had a different plan. Once this book is complete, my covenant to Him is fulfilled. This is more satisfying than you and I would ever imagine.

Printed and bound by PG in the USA

USA2019PGIL